EMERGENT AFRICA

Emergent Africa

SCIPIO

WITH A FOREWORD BY
PHILIP E. MOSELY

HOUGHTON MIFFLIN COMPANY BOSTON
THE RIVERSIDE PRESS CAMBRIDGE
1965

FOREWORD

EMERGENT AFRICA is a wise book. The word is one that I have chosen, after some hesitation, to express a quality of the author's mind and of his perspective on the development of Africa. As the author has observed at firsthand the movement of most of tropical Africa from colonial dependence to its new status in the world, he has caught for the reader the impact of many new and contradictory but independent aspirations. His study conveys a sense of the ways in which the new states are reaching out, in untested directions, to discover and define their identity both at home and in world affairs. Yet whatever is new must grow out of what is already there, and, despite its broad geographical sweep, this study leaves the reader with a feeling for the political and human assets with which the new entities are launching their careers. Just a word about the author. "Scipio" is, like his book, a wise person. In diplomacy he has never forgotten the responsibility of the scholar for searching out the main avenues of development. And in his academic pursuits he has not lost his sympathy for the diplomats, politicians, and economic doers who have to make many decisions day by day without the comforting assurance of the future historian about how things were bound to turn out. "Scipio" came to the field of African affairs after having made good use of both political and intellectual opportunities to understand the major powers in the postwar world. As an active participant in international affairs throughout the turbulent decade in which most of Africa achieved political independence he has paid equal and sensitive attention to the French and British connections with post-independence Africa and to African desires for

5

regional and continental unity. No study that I have seen has given as thoughtful an account of the contradictory strains within the foreign policies of the African states. Students of Africa and, more broadly, of independent Africa's role in regional and world affairs are greatly indebted to "Scipio" for sharing his firsthand observations and his many insights.

PHILIP E. MOSELY

The European Institute
Columbia University

CONTENTS

focus popular loyalties round themselves and away from colonial authorities . . . Para-statal functions — role of the Leader and of the educated élite . . . These parties as a force for stability after taking over power — the reasons for this . . . The usual division into traditional, popular-national and mass parties — but elements of each in most parties . . . Nature and importance of African influences . . . Influences from outside — colonial and revolutionary . . . The marginal importance in contemporary African contexts of parliamentary democracy and communism . . . "Bourgeois" instincts of the leadership — but managerial, not property-owning, bourgeoisie . . . Hence importance of party and state control and the primacy of politics

CONTENTS

PREFACE

T HE origin of this book is the growing need which I have felt to keep in focus the great devolution of power in tropical Africa from European to African hands. The political consequences of this transformation, both for the new African states themselves and for others, continue to manifest themselves. It is probably too early, and in any case I lack the qualifications, to see the effects on African society of this recovery of independence. But political and economic decisions must be made from day to day, and judgements formed, on the light of such understanding as we can bring to bear. I hope this book will be able to make some contribution towards the necessary process of producing a coherent picture of the problems that face the new governments. Each of the new countries has its individual personality, and its own aspirations and difficulties. These require to be studied and understood; though they are outside the scope of this book. But all of these new countries have much in common; and the context of these common elements is a new one since independence. Those concerned with political decisions in the new Africa cannot defer their study of this new context until the dust has settled. They must continually revise their picture of it as best they can.

The need for a new look at the scene as a whole—something more than an adjustment of the old picture that was valid for colonial times—is now clear. This book is an attempt to put forward tentatively some new generalizations about the African scene since Independence, to suggest how its leaders tend to think and feel, and to indicate how the problems of the new states came to be what they are. It will be for each student of the African scene who reads this book, in Africa or elsewhere, to test these generalizations and interpretations against his own experience and against events as they occur.

This book is not a chronological history of how independence came to Africa. Some good and many inferior ones are already available. Nor is the book an account, and still less a judgement, of the colonial period. It is only concerned with the legacy of colonialism in tropical Africa in so far as this affects the problems of the new states and governments since Independence, and particularly the outlook of their leaders. The effects of colonial rule after it has ceased to operate are not the whole story of colonialism. It seems to me personally that when the dust does settle and emotions have died down, both the intentions and the practices of colonial governments will come to be seen in a notably more favourable light than seems possible today in Africa, or even in the outside world as a whole. But that is as may be. Nor is the book designed to suggest policies for the various governments now concerned with Africa; or to offer them advice. It is too early to arrive at any judgement or verdict on how independence came to Africa. It is enough to see what general statements may be valid about the salient features of a rapidly changing scene.

I cannot list the large number of Africans from inside and outside the Commonwealth, and of others who know Africa well, whose conversations and correspondence have guided me towards a better understanding of Africa and its problems. I should like to express my thanks to them all. I trust it will seem less invidious to mention no names than to attempt any sort of list of those who have interpreted to me the inwardness of their changing continent.

When I speak of the new countries of tropical Africa, with which this book is concerned, I exclude the Arab countries of the northern littoral on the one hand, and the South African Republic, the High Commission Territories and Southern Rhodesia on the other. These are African countries too, and share some problems with the new states of the tropical area. But many of their traditions and problems are too different to include them in this survey. The Sudan is a borderline case; but much of what I have to say applies to it. There are also countries in the area which broadly speaking come into the same general context, though they are not new states. Ethiopia and Liberia have been independent for a long time: though Ethiopia had a brief experience of colonial occupation, and Liberia stands in a special relation to the United States. The Portuguese territories are not at present politically sovereign. A few British ones are still on the eve of a final transfer of power. Djibouti and the small Spanish possessions hardly affect the issue. "The new states of tropical Africa" must therefore be taken in this book to refer also, where appropriate, to these other states which either emerged some time ago or are still in an embryo stage. Since the phrase is a long one, I have sometimes abbreviated it to "African" as a convenient shorthand where the context seems clear.

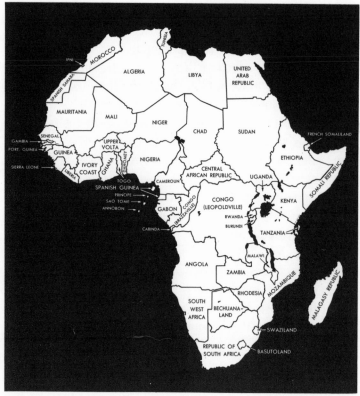

Chapter One

THE NEW CONTEXT IN
TROPICAL AFRICA

THE major change that has come over tropical Africa in the last few years, and which has produced a wholly new context for everything that has happened there, is the end of formal colonialism. Western European powers have ceased, or nearly ceased, to be responsible for administering the various individual blocks of territory into which their rivalries parcelled out Africa during the last eighty years or so. Three of the four West European governments mainly concerned, Britain, France and Belgium, have deemed the African populations of these countries ready not only to run their own local affairs but to manage a modern state; or at least have found it expedient to let them try.

The effects of this change, as they manifest themselves over time, cannot of course yet be seen, or forecast in detail. But it is perhaps already possible to discern the outlines of the new context, and to see the main factors that go to influence the building of African nations and shape their relations with the outside world. The compass of one short book is too small for a study of all the significant aspects of Africa's resumption of control over her own destinies. This book is not concerned with societies so much as states: not with the problems of individuals but of governments.

Though Europeans effectively administered most of Africa for only sixty years or so, this was a decisive period for Africa. It jerked the tropical zone of the continent summarily forwards into the modern world, much faster and in more unbalanced ways than could well have happened otherwise. But European influence did not begin with the period of effective occupation and administration. The impact of Europe was already felt in precolonial times.

Nor will it now come to an end because the European powers have ceased to govern Africa. Many of the connexions formed during colonial times, or even before, are likely to continue. Each of the European colonizing powers approached its task somewhat differently, and its rule has had discernibly different effects. By acquiring the equipment of modern statehood from one particular country, each African nation has learnt a specific European language and way of doing things, which familiarity makes it easier, if not inevitable, to maintain and adapt. (In this sense Liberia stands in the same relation to the United States as Sierra Leone to England and the Gabon to France.)

It is in the world of European domination and tutelage that the new African states have their roots. To understand their development it will therefore be necessary to look more closely at those aspects of the colonial legacy which are particularly likely to affect the new states after their attainment of political independence. I have tried to set out these aspects in the next chapter.

In the relations between these new countries and the rest of the world two main and largely conflicting factors stand out clearly. They are the elemental desire for independence and the almost desperate need for outside help. Their influence can also be seen in internal affairs, helping to mould the decisive process of building new nations. The basic importance of these two factors in modern Africa is obvious even to the casual observer of the scene; but their implications need careful examination.

In the long run the forming of the new nations themselves is what matters—the pattern established by a host of small practices and attitudes as well as by the basic decisions. For it is the character of the new states, rather than the expedients their governments adopt in relations with the outside world in the transitional period, that will ultimately determine their position in the comity of nations. Internally we may see the desire for independence and the need for outside help working together to some extent to produce strong governments.

After the departure of colonial authority, something must take its place which is not only capable of assuring order, but can also maintain and strengthen independence, and see that the foreign aid available is used for this purpose. Indeed without strong governments it is hard to see how new nations can be built in the absence of a unified political or popular tradition. For the new states whose international sovereignty has been recognized, and with which the outside world now has to deal, are not of course the multiplicity of little indigenous units, the shifting flux of tribal principalities that exercised local sovereignty in the period before colonial authority was established. They are new nation-states, that have come into being within the administrative boundaries established by the colonial powers for their own convenience. These boundaries may have been haphazard. They may have been decided by European statesmen in Europe ignorant of African conditions, and therefore sometimes divide ethnic and geographic units. But they provided during the colonial period the framework within which administration operated and modern political entities came into being. And the independent African nations today are essentially in the first instance the heirs of those entities.

This is so for two main reasons. The European governments for their part progressively handed over to Africans the administrative responsibility for running these new states, with their apparatus of modern government, their institutions and their communications. It is these units which the other nations of the world have recognized as internationally sovereign entities. And secondly, on the African side too loyalties crystallized out round parties and leaders within the boundaries of the European administrative units; and it was the government of these new units that the parties were designed to take over.

The key to the political evolution of these new countries towards independence has been the tendency towards the formation in each area of a single monolithic political party. This has been a genuine African development, not designed by the colonial authorities who, where they wanted political life at all, would have preferred a number of parties in each area, representing different views and interests. These African parties were designed to focus the loyalties of all the Africans in each new state; to weld them into a nation or as it were a new kind of tribe. The people came to obey the new party and to follow its leader even before independence. This development is so important for the understanding of the new states that it is studied in more detail in Chapter Three.

Power in the new African countries thus usually resides in a monolithic political party dominated by a leader or boss of at least semi-heroic proportions. Where this process was not complete by the time the colonial power handed over authority it has continued since. States like Senegal and Dahomey, and even the much troubled former Belgian Congo, are moving in this direction. So long as this system can maintain an adequate degree of stability and order, government seems likely to remain in the hands of civilian party machines. The prospects of a take over of power by the army, so common in other underdeveloped countries, seem less than elsewhere, though recent events in several states have shown how real the threat is. The armies in most of the new African countries are still rather embryonic and professionally inclined to obey the civilian authorities. But weakness and inefficiency of the civilian government, that lead the established military hierarchy to assumed power, or a group of young and revolutionary officers to stage a putsch, can easily develop in the new states of tropical Africa.

In the external field the longing of Africans to manage their own affairs, and to be free of European supervision, conflicts more directly with the urgent need of the new states for outside help. Of course the new African countries will be solicitous about their recently won independence. They will be anxious to extend it beyond the political self-government at home and in the world which they have so far achieved. For instance they will want to control their own economic life, which most of them do not yet do; and they will be correspondingly chary of anything which seems to them designed to perpetuate their present economic servitudes. But also, once independence has been obtained, both the leaders and the peoples of the new countries want material and social progress. And this the leaders know, or soon learn, they cannot achieve by themselves. And so the immediate and baffling problems of technological backwardness and economic inadequacy, discussed in Chapter Four, complicate the desire for economic emancipation and often overlay it.

The main external question which now confronts these new independent African states is what their relations with the world of Western civilization and advanced technology should be. And within this general question the most insistent aspect of it is the relationship with the former metropolitan power. For there can be no question of these new countries, these polities forged by the colonial occupation and given a taste of the technological revolution, reverting to the smaller African societies of the period before colonial rule. And in most cases the former colonial country is better able than other countries to supply much of the essential outside aid, especially in expert personnel familiar with the local scene. So the process of decolonization is complicated by the desire for technical and economic advance.

The prevailing African pattern of firm rule by a single party headed by a hero-boss has an important consequence for the relations of the new states with the outside world, in this key issue and in others. The Leader, accepted and acclaimed by the party and the people for other reasons than his foreign policy, is comparatively free from domestic pressures in the arrangements he makes with other governments. There is always, of course, a general desire not to depend too closely after independence on the former colonial master. But the rate of dissociation, the speed of the process of weaning, is largely a matter for the boss and his immediate henchmen to decide. Even more so are the arrangements with other sources of aid, the degree of association with the United States or Israel or the Communist bloc. The surprisingly varying decisions in this whole field, even between states with similar party structures and similar needs, and the extent to which individual states can change or reverse their decisions, illustrate both the political nature of these decisions, and the remarkable freedom of action of the individual leaders on issues of major importance for the future character of their nations. In general the choices are determined both by political predilection and by expediency. The nub of the matter for African leaders is where to strike a balance between material advantage and the deep, emotional desire for disengagement.

So far as the outside world is concerned, there is much continuity in the pattern of trade and aid, though the virtual monopoly of the administering power in colonial times is giving way to a more diffused pattern. The important new factor for those engaged in African trade and development is that the crucial decisions are being made increasingly by Africans. The new states are now coming into the position where they can decide for themselves what their relations should be with their former colonial masters and also with other advanced countries. This is a gradual, not a sudden, unfolding of opportunity. It is not something that happened on Independence Morning. Relations and contacts with other powers increased during the period before the attainment of international sovereignty. And for some time afterwards there are many restraints and limitations, imposed both by specific agreements and by the dictates of self-interest. But though the process is gradual, the new states of tropical Africa are finding themselves increasingly able to control and to diversify their relations with the technically advanced countries. The problems of trade and aid, and the political character of African decisions about them, form the subject of Chapter Five.

Another factor to play a large part in determining the operation of the new governments is the dearth of Africans with adequate educational qualifications. The crucial decisions about the nature of the new states very largely rest with the small élite of Africans who have so far received a modern education. This concentration is reinforced by the tendency towards single authoritarian parties. Moreover, if the African states are to solve successfully the main problems that face them today, such as the achievement of more complete independence and "Africanization", the struggle against technological backwardness, malnutrition and disease, and the reduction of their present need for outside aid, they must urgently train more of their own citizens to assume these tasks with a sense of responsibility and to discharge them competently. A great increase in modern education, at all levels, is not merely the advice of foreign experts. It is the general desire of the peoples of the new states, who see in education a principal means of personal betterment. It is the set policy of almost all the new governments. And since no African state has either the men or the money to carry out such a policy quickly and effectively alone, it figures prominently in the aid programmes of outside governments and institutions. The immediate benefits of the wide dissemination of modern technical education in tropical Africa are clear in administrators' minds. The long-term effects are incalculable. Universal education in the most advanced states of Western Europe is scarcely more than a century old. I have therefore devoted Chapter Six to the problems of education and of the educated élite.

The relations of the new governments with their neighbours and with the rest of the world are not confined to these technical and economic problems, important though they are in the eyes of the African leaders. The origins of foreign policy can be found in that very re-assertion of Africa's distinctness, of the alien nature of the colonizing power, that are the mainspring of independence. These emotions colour the dealings of African governments with their former masters and with other donors. They also largely determine the familiar solidarity of African governments with each other; especially on issues that affect all Africans, and most of all on ending alien domination everywhere on the continent. They affect the desire of the new nations to dissociate themselves from non-African quarrels, which expresses itself in neutralism; and the desire to make their countries known and respected in the world. These are issues on which expediency may temper the actions of individual statesmen. But they are issues on which, broadly speaking, Africans think alike and on which the foreign policies of the new states are more or less the same.

The examination of the origins of foreign policy in Chapter Seven completes the material for a stocktaking, in the following chapter, of the way in which the new states have evolved since independence. This assessment of the general position may provide us with some clues about what to expect in the near future. For this purpose the colonial era, though it is only now ending and has fundamentally transformed Africa, is a quite inadequate guide.

In some ways the end of colonial rule means that the relationship of tropical Africa with European and other outside powers and their citizens will revert to a pattern more like that of a hundred years ago. A great deal of the technical skill and expertise required to develop the new African countries will still have to come from more advanced lands. But the doors will be open once more to all whom the Africans wish to allow in. And those who bring in this expertise—the governments, international organizations, public institutions, private enterprises—will have to be allowed to do so on terms that seem to them to justify the undertaking. In other words, there will have to be a bargain struck each time between the new country and those who bring in the skills, that makes it seem worth while to both sides. In such bargains psychological factors, including the sense of responsibility of the more advanced countries towards the less advanced, will play their part. No doubt some of the new governments will prefer to obtain these skills from some sources rather than others; though for reasons which we shall examine none of them is likely to want to depend too exclusively on any one outside power, and more especially not on the former colonial master. But it seems that few Africans will want to go beyond diversification of their contacts, to sever all connexion with the former colonial power. On the contrary, the signs are that in many—perhaps most—African countries the links formed in the colonial period will remain stronger than others.

There also seems to be a fair prospect that there will not

be overmuch rivalry or jealousy, among the Western nations at least, in regard to what they and their nationals do in African countries. A century ago the tendency of European enterprise and activity in tropical Africa was towards monopoly, with exclusive privileges and obligations in certain areas, and a corresponding acceptance of exclusion from others; which finally led to the assumption of colonial authority. Now we may perhaps expect the dissolution of these monopoly positions, and the gradual establishment or resumption of connexions between all the new African states and those countries outside Africa which may have something to offer.

Subject peoples, obliged to study their masters, come to understand or at least to feel the motives of these masters very clearly. And if sometimes they appear even to impartial listeners to dwell especially on the less noble and altruistic reasons for colonization, this is perhaps partly because the picture presented by spokesmen for the colonial power are naturally weighted the other way. Miss Margery Perham, in her recent Reith Lectures, sums up very objectively the range of motives which impelled Britain to undertake colonial activity in Africa as follows. "We can identify five main purposes which led Britain to build up an Empire. . . . There was the economic purpose, mainly the expansion of trade. . . . This created the further purpose of security. . . . Emigration provided another purpose. . . . The supreme purpose of Empire was the attainment and enjoyment of power and prestige. . . . There slowly grew a fifth purpose, the challenging ideal of philanthropy, and this alone saw the interests of the ruled as equal, if not indeed superior, to those of their rulers." A similar list by a Frenchman or a Portuguese would give prominence to the purpose of cultural and even religious assimilation, the mission to romanize. The French authorities usually listed high among their objectives the recruitment of overseas manpower for their army, which is a special form of security.

If these and perhaps other motives impelled the powers of Western Europe towards Africa in colonial times, is it possible to say what are likely to be the interests of a much wider range of outside countries in the new dispensation? What types of bargain are likely to be struck in future?

One of my purposes in trying to sift the available evidence about the forces which determine political and economic life in the new states of tropical Africa has been the diplomatic one, in the wider sense, of understanding more clearly what the nature of their relations with the outside world are likely to be. I hope that this book, by marshalling the main factors involved, will help to a small extent the process now actively taking place on the international stage of working out the part which the new Africa is to play there. I have therefore attempted in the last chapter to indicate what may be tropical Africa's place in the world; and what the rest of the world, and particularly the West, may expect in its relations with this concert of new states.

Chapter Two

SOME ASPECTS OF THE
COLONIAL LEGACY

THE new states of tropical Africa have inherited a great deal from colonial rule, including their very existence as political entities. This legacy has been described so often and so competently, both by those who are inclined to magnify the achievements of colonial rule and those who are inclined to belittle it, that there is no need to make a comprehensive survey again. It will be enough to pick out certain aspects of this inheritance which are particularly relevant to the theme of this book.

When studying the colonial legacy of the new African states, it is important to bear in mind how brief the effective period of colonial administration was over most of tropical Africa. The parcelling out of the interior of the continent dates from 1880. Before that only a very small part of tropical Africa was under European administration. In West Africa there had been a number of European trading settlements for centuries and they exercised some influence beyond their administrative limits; but only the British in the Gold Coast and the French in Senegal had colonies of any significant extent. In Angola and Mozambique the Portuguese traded far into the interior but without administering it. North of Mozambique there were no European posts in East Africa even on the coast.

Thereafter the "scramble" for Africa divided the continent into some forty colonial territories. However, this partition took place more on paper than on the spot. Once the colonizing powers were satisfied that the territories assigned to them would not be occupied by rival European powers, they were in no great hurry to occupy and administer the remoter areas. "Nothing", say Professor Oliver and Professor Fage in their Short History of Africa, "so well demonstrates the element of unreality in the scramble for Africa as the 35 years of almost total obscurity which followed the limelight of partition . . . the colonial powers had partitioned Africa as an insurance for the future, not because thay had any present plans for its exploitation." Effective colonial rule and peaceful administration were not established until the turn of the century; that is sixty years ago. Many areas were only brought under settled European government at a still later date. At first, moreover, the European powers were not prepared to spend much money or send out many men to govern any but the most valuable areas. Most Africans, it seems safe to say, were not much affected by colonial rule in its early stages. The real and profound changes in the life of tropical Africa produced by colonialism (as distinct from contacts with Europeans in the pre-colonial eras) have largely taken place in the last forty years.

There were distinctions, of course, between the policies of the different colonial powers. The French purpose was essentially to romanize; to establish overseas provinces of France; to assimilate first a small élite and then more gradually the whole population; to provide a French administration in the new provinces; and to bring African Frenchmen to participate in the government of the Empire, both in the provinces and at the centre. Except in the areas of white settlement (Kenya and the Rhodesias) Britain colonized more lightly than France.[1] She provided the territories under her rule with much of the technical equipment of a modern state, including a working knowledge of an advanced world language; but African administrations, languages and values were more respected, and adapted for modern use. Africans were trained for eventual "self-government" of their own territories, not to think of themselves as black Englishmen playing their part in the government of the Empire as a whole. In the colonial period the Portuguese system came to resemble the French. It aimed (as it still does) to assimilate and romanize the "ultramarine provinces of Portugal". But this aim has been pursued with considerably less vigour than the great French outpouring of effort and money; and it incorporates traditions of its own inherited from centuries of active contact with Africa before 1880. The Belgian administration was in essentials rather like the British; though more concerned with economic development and less with preparing Africans for self-government. These distinctions need to be borne in mind when examining the colonial heritage of the new African states. But they make less difference than might be supposed. In essence the experience of colonialism was much the same all over tropical Africa; and so is the range of African reactions to it.

The most important contribution of colonialism to tropical Africa is that the new countries which have emerged have been endowed with a tradition of order, over wider areas than in pre-colonial times. They have acquired an idea of government as something especially

[1] That is, Britain made less effort to refashion African societies to conform with a European model.

concerned with maintaining order, and determined to take effective measures to do so. The European form of government was welcomed by many Africans for this reason, as Hobbes welcomed Leviathan. Around this grid of order the arts of peace could flourish, and especially those arts introduced from outside. With this order there are associated in the minds of some, freedom of movement, escape from tribal and traditional restraints, and individual advance protected not by tribal solidarity but by state law. Even a cursory glance at the new states shows how well most of their leaders appreciate this aspect of their legacy.

Along with this new and wider order, colonial rule bequeathed to the peoples it governed opportunities for a more individual existence. It introduced a money economy, with cities, plantations and mines, and cash crops for those who did not wish to go so far afield. Those Africans who have come into contact with these new opportunities have found themselves inculcated with new values and new ideas. Of course there were towns, and Empires, and wide-ranging trade before the brief period of white colonization, all across the northern and eastern stretches of tropical Africa; and no doubt there would have been such opportunities, to some extent, without the establishment of colonial rule. But not in the same measure, surely; as Ethiopia and Liberia show. The additional degree of emancipation from traditional restraints is a legacy of colonialism. And within the ambit of colonialism its distribution was made uneven and its effects limited by two factors: white settlement and indirect rule.

White men settled in Africa only where the climate and the economic prospects seemed propitious. Where they did strike roots, the settlers wanted, more even than white traders or missionaries, a government which would protect their interests and provide them with the facilities such as communications which they needed. Soon they wanted to take the government of the territory concerned into their own hands, so as to run it in their own interests, which they felt were not clearly appreciated by the distant imperial government or even its local agents. In such areas the white settlers, like the mining and other white enterprises throughout tropical Africa, required African labour; and on the whole were glad to teach this African labour the skills needed to perform the unfamiliar and fairly complex tasks required even at the lower levels of modern farming, mining and industry. The situation was complicated by the immigration of Asians into the areas of white settlement, usually under private European sponsorship. Most of these Asians came as labourers, and they and their descendants built themselves by diligence and thrift into a petty middle class which in effect prevented many Africans from rising to positions which they might have otherwise learned to occupy. Neither the settlers nor even the governments of such territories needed or wanted to train Africans to assume responsibility for the higher levels of administration, to represent the territory in parliaments or to staff the educated professions. So it is that in the Republic of South Africa, to take a classic example from outside the tropical zone, the level of African income per head is far higher than anywhere else in Africa south of the Sahara; and in spite of the severe limitations imposed by law and custom on the employment of Africans in the more skilled jobs, the general level of African skills is also notably higher; but in administrative and governmental experience as well as in the educated professions the Africans of the Republic lag behind those of much poorer but more purely African states.

The other limiting factor was indirect rule. In the widest sense this meant administering African territories at least to some extent through existing African authorities; and so by its nature, it restrained the emancipation and detribalization of individual Africans. In its classic form it was a British policy: born of the British desire to make Africa safe for certain British interests, as economically and smoothly as seemed practicable; and the lack of desire to turn Africans into overseas Britons.[1] The Belgians, without proclaiming indirect rule as a policy in certain areas, as the British did, proceeded very cautiously in detribalizing African societies under their rule. The romanizing French and Portuguese have also used the system, though less as a matter of deliberate purpose than the British or the Belgians. In their colonies indirect rule remained an expedient, a provisional way of administering an area or a tribe through its own African authorities, or at least allowing these to survive alongside the colonial administrative apparatus, until such time as a greater degree of assimilation seemed practicable.

Indirect rule did not leave, and could not have left, African institutions and values as they were. Many able

---

[1] A senior British official once described Indirect Rule to me as "born of nothing else than the dictates of common sense and the local situation and the parsimony of the British Treasury, combined with the British Government's lack of interest in running or paying for an Empire". These are indeed precisely the factors that dominate policy in the absence of the romanizing impulse.

studies have been made of the intentional and unintentional changes produced in individual African societies even under systems of indirect rule which allowed them largely to manage their own affairs. These changes have enabled traditional African societies to adapt themselves without dissolution, and with their traditional loyalties often largely intact, to the exigencies of the modern world. In one sense they represent a half-way house between full colonialism and what might have been the course of evolution in tropical Africa if formal colonial rule had not been established there. But certainly in areas of indirect rule individual Africans were less emancipated psychologically, socially or technically, less made into individual and unsatisfied members of the modern world, than in areas of direct rule and progressive assimilation. One effect of this has been that the more restless and thrusting spirits in areas of indirect rule tended to leave the tribal restraints which chafed them, and to seek wider individual opportunities outside, especially in the towns.

The most active centres for the dissemination of new Western skills and for emancipation from traditional tribal responsibilities and restraints were the white man's towns. There were large African cities before the colonial era; some of which retain their former importance. Where these cities were the centres of Christian or Moslem kingdoms like Axum or Kano, they disseminated within an African traditional framework the skills and the civilization drawn ultimately from the Mediterranean. But the white man's towns were something new. They were created to serve his needs—commerce, administration, mining. They drew Africans as individuals, detribalized them, taught them new skills and new values. However

33

much African traditional ways and even traditional authorities might continue in the countryside, in the towns Africans were sucked into the white man's world, and sucked into it as inferiors. As they realized something of the scope and the possibilities of European civilization, so they also came to understand that its purposes were not theirs, and to feel that they were being exploited for ends other than their own. These feelings were reinforced by the loneliness of the African townships, the sense of being lost and uprooted, away from the reassuring pattern and order of tribal life. Brought continually face to face with the power, the comforts, the advantages enjoyed by the Europeans, they wanted these advantages for themselves. And they wanted to end the discrimination which relegated Africans to an inferior status.

The manifold contacts with the agents of Western civilization—the colonial authorities, the missionaries, the traders and settlers, the armies—gradually produced in the colonial societies of Africa a Western educated class or élite. These élites were recruited from a wide spectrum of backgrounds. They were the main channel through which European ideas spread into Africa. They were the main advocates and organizers of African independence and the end of colonial rule. And it is they who largely govern and fashion the new African states of today.

To many Africans living under European authority, and conscious that this authority derived from superior skills, the individual way upward and out of the morass of humiliating inferiority has seemed to lie through learning what the white man knew. Education was the great emancipator. It could lift an able and determined African out of a communal tribe or a city slum, and give him a professional standing in the hierarchy introduced by the Europeans. As the colonial system established itself, so the demand for African education grew. The belief in the advantages of education, and the desire for more, was instilled into the active elements of the African population in colonial times, and is today a significant colonial legacy in the new independent states.

So by contact with Europeans, by precept and by example, in school and out of school, a small élite of Western-educated Africans was gradually formed, distinguished from the rest of the African population by greater familiarity with European civilization. These élites were of heterogeneous origin. They ranged from the children of rulers and other traditional authorities, educated in order to assume administrative responsibilities, through the employees of European companies and individuals and the brighter products of missionary and government schools, to the more wholly detribalized descendants of emancipated slaves and people of mixed blood. (Both these last groups have played an impressive part in the development of West African society in particular.)

These Westernized Africans did not in any sense form a compact or united group. The degree of assimilation varied enormously. Different elements of Western civilization were learnt, from the most intellectual to the most mechanical; and these elements were combined with an enormous range of widely differing African traditions and standards. Many of the most assimilated Africans held high positions in the colonial or pre-colonial established order, and were firmly conservative; while others with no inherited or appointed position were frankly revolutionary and have sometimes remained so even when they have since established themselves in positions of authority. This difference between the old and the new élite seemed fundamental to colonial administrators and to many students of Africa affairs. But important though it is, it should not be exaggerated. What all the élites have in common is their acquisition, to a greater or less extent, of Western techniques and Western values. Largely as a result of colonial rule, virtually every African leader today occupies a position somewhere in the scale of this Westernized élite.

But though these Westernized Africans acquired Western values of one kind or another to a greater or lesser degree, and sometimes became so attached to Western civilization that they have felt spiritually more at home in Europe than among less assimilated Africans, this did not normally carry with it any deep loyalty to the political interests of the colonial power. Indeed almost all Africans, whether conservative or revolutionary in their views about their own society, were attracted by European beliefs about national independence, liberty and the equality of peoples. During the Second World War Africans had seen right-wing nationalists and left-wing Marxists in the Western world agreed in resisting domination and exploitation by an alien conqueror. What we should today call African national loyalties began to form in their own minds.

This was the case even, and sometimes especially, among those Africans who seemed most assimilated by the West. In British territories educated Africans were not encouraged or taught to think of themselves as Overseas Englishmen, provincial members of a European cultural and political system. Self-government, however distinct in practice, was always held out as the ultimate goal of the British colonial Empire in Africa. So in British territories African loyalties were taken for granted. Affection for Britain, and a readiness to support her, there might sometimes be. An understanding of the value after independence of Commonwealth membership, a desire to retain a common sovereign, there certainly were. But loyalty is the wrong term to describe the feelings of such people towards the colonial power.

The position in the French colonies was less clear. The French until recently thought in terms of assimilation and romanization. The Portuguese, officially, still do. Consequently there were French Africans who sincerely thought of themselves as Frenchmen. What other prospect could compare, for a French African évolué, with a seat in the Legislature in Paris? The original purpose of such people was to remove the disabilities, both in law and in fact, which relegated African Frenchmen to an inferior status. But in fact, as the prospect of self-government drew nearer and Africans became more conscious of their "separate destiny", most of these assimilated Africans felt the pull of other and stronger loyalties (see Chapter Seven). Save for a numerically tiny number of exceptions, these French and Portuguese Africans have absorbed, along with other elements of European civilization, a very European sense of national consciousness and pride, the desire to be masters in their own house and the belief in the legitimacy of this desire. Today the resolve to be independent of European tutelage, the nationalist rejection of assimilation into an alien Imperial system, stands out in all the new African countries as a major and characteristic legacy of the colonial period.

Perhaps the most typical features of this national consciousness, the desire for independence, is resentment at
being treated as inferior. This is partly the familiar reaction against racial discrimination. There is a natural
resentment against the colour bar, official or unofficial,
from which all colonial societies in tropical Africa suffered.
Africans were made aware at every turn that almost
all Europeans—and Asians—felt themselves superior to
Africans as a whole. The highly civilized exceptions—a
traditional ruler treated with ceremonial respect, or a
professional man with a French wife practising law or
medicine in a large city—knew and felt keenly what the
world thought about their fellow-countrymen.

This African resentment was greatly aggravated by the
acute and shaming sense that in so many things which
seem to matter—in education and mechanical competence, and indeed in the whole tradition of achievement in
the arts and sciences that make up civilization—most
Africans were indeed woefully backward. Save in very
exceptional cases Africans did not of course feel that their
people were innately inferior. As human beings they felt
equal to those who despised them on account of technical
backwardness, and indeed superior in many of the human
virtues which their conquerors preached. Islam where it
existed was also a source of spiritual independence of the
white man and of personal pride. The most advanced
among the African élite, like M. Leopold Senghor and
Mr Jomo Kenyatta, came in different ways to see that
African societies had real cultural values of their own, and
that if these were fostered instead of being distorted and
suppressed, *négritude* could make a distinctive contribution to world civilization. What had to be learnt was

essentially technical, they told themselves. And it could be learnt from the French or the British, just as the primitive Gauls and Britons had learnt it from the Romans, the Greeks and the Jews. It was a daunting task, especially to those who saw the long perspectives of history. However much damage colonial rule may have done to the development of African civilization, even the semi-legendary past did not seem to most educated Africans much more promising than the inadequate present. It was clear that in practice almost everything needed to be learnt from the outside.

To the less educated élite the problem seemed simpler. The white man had various amenities and sources of power: the cars, the houses, the guns, and the technical know-how that went with them. He had these things because the whites were the bosses. These things could be given or taught to Africans, just as they were to individual Europeans. Some Africans had them already. It was just a question of who was boss. The concept of a technological society capable of producing these things for itself, or at least of maintaining them when acquired from outside, discussed in Chapter Four, is even now understood only by a small and thoughtful minority among the numerically small élite. The great majority of Africans who saw in colonial times how the white man lived in their midst, and the advantages he enjoyed—in a word the benefits of technological progress—wanted these benefits for themselves. And they felt that the white man was denying them to Africans. Those who visited the modern world were impressed and usually resentful at the contrast between the standards which their colonial masters maintained for their own people at home and the vastly lower ones they allowed to continue in Africa. The end of colonial rule would go far to solve the problem: at any rate for the élite who could then hope to step into the white man's shoes.

The end of colonial subjection thus appeared to an increasing number of African leaders to be the first necessity. If the Africans could now regain control of their own destinies, so both reason and deeply felt emotion suggested; if instead of doing the bidding of alien and contemptuous masters and seeing their economies distorted for alien ends, they could apply themselves to African ends, under African direction, then they could recover their self-respect and improve their material position. Of course, extensive foreign help would still be necessary: foreign experts would have to be hired in large numbers until Africans could be trained. Some thought that perhaps even a fairly lengthy period of close association with the former colonial power would prove wise. Others argued, or felt emotionally, that a new African country could do better elsewhere. Even if the economic and political price was stiff, colonial rule had taught them how necessary foreign assistance was. But the Africans must be masters; and the foreign experts must carry out African purposes, instead of giving orders as before.

We have so far been concerned with what may be called the political and personal effects of colonial rule on the new countries of Africa as they emerge from its authority. Equally important is the economic legacy of the colonial period. This affects both the commerce between Africa and the outside world, which is largely what brought the Europeans to establish spheres of influence in Africa in the first place; and also the development of Africa's resources on the spot.

The main economic effect of colonialism was to stimu-late the production of those products which the imperial economy could use. As a result it left the new African states with rapidly developed but distorted economies. The consequences of this are examined in Chapter Five. But it is first necessary to understand why the position now inherited by the African states came into being.

The trade of tropical Africa with Europe in the days before the establishment of colonial rule, and the smaller trade with the Moslem world from Morocco to India, was conducted by visitors from the outside. These traders came to tropical Africa in order to obtain the particular commodities they wanted; and to pay for them (where they did not take them) by whatever goods the Africans would accept that could be provided most cheaply. Since in fact African manufacturing skills were, then as now, much lower than those of the European or the Moslem world, there was a regular and eager demand in Africa for a wide range of goods. The problem for the Africans was rather to find commodities like gold, ivory or slaves which the foreign visitors wanted in exchange. The whole of the European slave trade in Africa, which is perhaps the most horrifying chapter in the annals of modern commerce, was based on the sale of slaves by other Africans to white slavers in return for goods which these Africans wanted.

Let us make no mistake about this. So far as the Africans were concerned and leaving out the motives of those who bought the slaves, the basis of the African slave trade, both westwards to the Europeans and in so far as it

was trade at all Eastwards to the Arabs too, was the insistent African hunger for the manufactures of the more
advanced civilizations. Those Europeans who wanted to
suppress the slave trade in the nineteenth century saw
that the key to doing so was to discover other African
commodities than slaves which it would pay European
traders to ship out of Africa in return for the goods they
shipped in. And this is what, in the years between the
outlawing of the slave trade by the more civilized European powers and the partition of Africa which ushered
in the colonial period, was beginning to happen. Pre-
colonial trade with Africa was not just an exploitation
by outsiders of African backwardness. It was character-
ized also by African buying and selling to traders from
the developed world a few specialized commodities which
the outside world wanted in order to obtain in exchange
the general range of goods which the developed world
could manufacture and African could not. In colonial
times the European countries continued to look to Africa
for a range of specialized products that their economies
could use in return for goods not traditionally produced
in Africa. The *laisser-faire* economic views of the period
assigned to governments the role of maintaining order,
providing such facilities as communications and courts of
justice, and assuming some degree of responsibility for
matters such as education and health. It was for private
enterprise to produce, or induce others to produce, the
goods it required. The distinguishing feature of the
colonial system was that this private enterprise usually
became very largely the enterprise of the colonial power.
It operated under imperial protection and sometimes to
the virtual exclusion of enterprise from other developed

countries. But in essence it was much the same as in pre-colonial times.

The economies of tropical African colonies were not left to develop primarily in order to satisfy their own essential needs, and by means of slowly acquiring a range of local skills based on the use of local resources, as the more self-sufficient economies of European nations, for instance, had done. They were stimulated more rapidly by the arrival from outside of capital and expertise, under the protection of the colonial power, in order to satisfy the specialized requirements of a distant and much more developed economy. This phenomenon was not, of course, limited to colonial territories. The concepts of free trade and economic specialization postulated that each area should concentrate on those commodities which it could produce best and most cheaply, and import from other areas what it could not produce so well as they. This condition was never realized between the developed economies for a number of reasons, including the fear of undue dependence on the outside world for strategic essentials. Developing countries like the United States and Russia took particular pains to protect their infant industries from the competition of cheaper goods from more developed economies. But between the different areas of a single economy specialization became increasingly the rule as internal barriers were removed and communication became easier. And colonial territories were regarded as forming a single economy with the "mother country."

The inclusion of colonial territories in an imperial economy in this way was not unnatural or uneconomic. The colonial system had been established by seafaring

European powers, largely in the wake of their traders; and it was usually cheaper to move goods, especially bulky ones, by sea than by land. In the Age of Expansion nobody suggested that an economy or an Empire should only expand across land frontiers, like the United States or Russia, and even in retrospect this idea was dismissed as "the salt-water fallacy". This specialization developed the colonial territories of European powers faster than would otherwise have been the case. But the form of this development made the colonial economies increasingly dependent on that of the developed colonial power, and discouraged the attainment of the minimum degree of self-sufficiency, the minimum of diversity, which seems necessary for a state to stand on its own feet in the world of today. Devices such as imperial preference, guaranteed markets and artificially high prices for certain cash crops, which were designed to increase the self-sufficiency of the great imperial trading systems, further stimulated and concentrated production in their African territories.

Now the new African countries, wishing to end their insulation from the rest of the world inside an imperial system, find themselves politically independent, but heirs to specialized and perhaps "greenhouse" economies whose activity has been largely concentrated on producing sometimes only one or two specialized commodities for export. These commodities have in recent times tended to be either agricultural, like cotton, coffee, groundnuts, palm oil and tobacco; or mineral ores, especially iron and copper, and precious substances like gold and diamonds.

The main distinguishable development in tropical Africa in colonial times, then, was the need of the metropolitan power. But though the stimulus produced a lopsided economy and encouraged the production of raw materials rather than processing and manufacturing, development was much faster and more extensive than it would have been under alternative systems. This was partly because colonial administration made it practicable to bring in both private capital and skills at what seemed much less risk than in countries outside colonial control, and also because the colonial government provided what is now called a much better infrastructure of communications and other facilities. This increased rate of development is especially visible in the few areas of white settlement in tropical Africa. Where white men came to live in considerable numbers not simply in order to trade or to organize mines, but to farm and engage in other settled activities, they redoubled the effects of administrative colonialism. African societies were disrupted, and Africans were often denied what seemed to them a legitimate place in the new order; but the rate of economic progress in such areas, often from very low levels, and the increase in wealth and technical skills of many Africans, have of recent years been more spectacular there than elsewhere in the continent.

Chapter Three

THE MAKE-UP OF
AFRICAN POLITICAL PARTIES

IT has now come to be a commonplace that the new
states of tropical Africa tend to be dominated by single
political parties, which try to establish control of all or
most aspects of public life. The basic purpose of these parties during the last stages of colonial rule was to crystallize
popular loyalties round themselves instead of round the
colonial authorities and the institutions provided by
them. This was no less true when the party decided, for
tactical reasons, to make use of this or that piece of colonial
constitutional machinery. For the aim was not mere dissidence. It was to forge a new moral authority within a
new and generally accepted community, against the day
when it could take over power from the colonial authority. To establish this new community, and to bring the
mass of the people to regard the party as Us and not as
just another Them, effective links were needed running
from the party leadership down to every village and township, and back. These links had to be capable not only of
galvanizing the mass of the people and moulding their
opinions, but also of keeping the leadership aware of, and
sensitive to, popular hopes and fears. Thus it was necessary to go beyond the familiar parades, rallies and tam-
tams, the flags and the emblems, the party membership
cards and subscriptions, the political manifestations, the
strikes, and the many other techniques for putting fire
into the faithful. The party must assume so far as

possible, and in anticipation of taking over power, the functions of a state. The authority of the part must extend beyond the state's moral functions to its physical ones. So we find the party engaged in a whole range of para-statal activities. Such parties had their own treasury; their own loans to the needy; even their own marketing machinery for important crops (Mr Krobo Edusei once called his party's Cocoa Purchasing Company "the atom bomb of the C.P.P."). They had their own systems of legal aid and of citizen's advice. They had their own systems of maintaining discipline, of intimidation and enforcement—their own police forces, with boycotts and occasional arson to bring backsliders or collaborators with the colonial power to heel. But the two main and characteristic techniques used by these parties were, and after independence still remain, mass indoctrination by disciplined party militants, and the conscious building up of the image and personality of a leader or Hero. This broadly familiar process has been well and comprehensively analysed and described in Mr Thomas Hodgkin's *African Political Parties* and Professor Immanuel Wallerstein's *Africa: the Politics of Independence*, to quote only two outstanding examples, one by a British and one by an American scholar.

The leaders, the "charismatic heroes" who come to symbolize their peoples (as well as those bosses who achieve something less than this symbolic status), get their start in life because of their Western education. This is an essential qualification; though they may also be distinguished from their fellows in other ways also, such as by being members of hereditary chiefly families. They then work their way to the top largely by virtue of their capacity for leadership and their organizing ability. Once

47

their position has been established they become the recognized leaders of their party and ultimately of their new nation. Their authority is not derived from the policies they pursue once in power, and is to a great extent independent of them. These policies are determined by their own political outlook; by their personal loyalties and rivalries; by the pressure of other powerful figures in the party machine or governmental coalition; and by the political beliefs and aspirations of their more politically conscious followers. But their powers to carry these policies out is derived from their personal magnetism and their hold over their party machine. So we find that leaders of different temperament and subject to different pressures tackle the same problems in ways that are very diverse.

The majority of the people accept such men as leaders and follow them, often with resolute loyalty, because they have won acceptance as the boss. The majority acquiesce in the political course the leader adopts, even when it would not otherwise meet with general enthusiasm or even agreement. This is naturally less true of matters which touch individual Africans very directly; willingness to let the leader decide is especially marked over issues like foreign relations which are beyond most people's ken. But over the whole field it remains broadly true that the policies of the leader are accepted because of him, rather than he because of his policies. Such a leader has inherited something of the mantle of the traditional chief, as he also has something of the mantle of the colonial Governor. So too authority in Europe in former times was invested in the Prince. *Cujus regio, ejus religio.*

In the final stages of the transition to independence, and

after, such organized machines of mass loyalty represent the obvious and stable alternative to chaos and civil strife on the one hand and military dictatorship on the other. Of course, the change from opposition to formal authority brings with it certain changes of emphasis and technique. Above all, party activities are no longer attuned to creating solidarity in dissidence, but solidarity and cohesion in support of the new authority. But the party machine and the leader remain the essential means of achieving this. Wallerstein aptly says: "The Party and the Hero can be seen as a pair of surgical clamps which hold the state together while the bonds of affection and legitimation grow."

This transition naturally takes place more smoothly if there is a long period of gradual transference of power: if the colonial authorities accept and facilitate the devolution. Where such a party has already been allowed to climb politically into the saddle well before independence, it gains experience of government in the fields open to it, receives longer administrative training, and a dislocating breach is avoided. This assumption of power by the party puts a premium on orderliness and authority, even though opposition to the remaining positions of colonial control may continue. Hodgkin lists two other main reasons for the "constitutional bias" of even the more radical African dominant parties. They are predisposed by their structure and by the middle-class outlook of their leaders to seek power by legal or at least non-violent means where these are available. And they are "modernist" and authority conscious enough to fear tribal and uncontrolled violence. One might say that even more fundamentally the essential para-statal function of such parties is to create an alternative system of order and authority, based on popular identification and loyalty. This becomes more manifest after independence when the party becomes, as Waller-stein says, a clamp holding the society together while the legitimacy of the new order comes to be accepted. The fact that such political parties have during the colonial period been in opposition, even violently, against the colonial authority should not obscure their essential nature. It takes forceful repression by the colonial power, and the absence of any visible prospect of attaining inde-pendence by moderate methods, to convert such a party from reliance on civil disobedience touched up with minor clashes, and turn it into a military machine for con-ducting partisan warfare.

It is customary to see such single and monopolistic parties as ranging in composition from those which at the outset largely reproduced the traditional African pattern of authority, like the *Kabaka Yekka* in Uganda, the North-ern People's Congress in Nigeria, or the *Union Progressiste Mauritanienne* in Mauritania, through "popular national" parties speaking for the Bakongo or the Yorubas, to mass parties aiming to speak for all Africans within the boun-daries of a given colonial territory, like the Convention People's Party in Ghana or the Tanganyika African National Union. The two last categories of party are usually regarded as led by the uprooted intelligentsia created by the impact of Westernization, and animated by an ideology largely derived from the West.

This pattern seems to me largely schematic. It is useful for purposes of analysis. But most parties in practice have a more complex make-up, and many elements are com-bined in varying degrees. Almost all of them have much that is African about them: characteristics that can be classed as "pre-colonial" even though not faithfully traditional. Almost all, too, have characteristics derived from the facts of colonial rule. And there are few who have not learnt at least some of their ideas and their techniques from outside, usually from progressive movements in Europe. It is worth examinining these influences in more detail.

The African influences are themselves of many kinds. In most areas pre-colonial systems of government and authority survive in varying degrees. The Emirates of Northern Nigeria, or the interlacustrine Bantu kingdoms of Uganda or Burundi, do not depend for their political influence simply on a tribal or national cohesion. To a large extent they command the loyalties, and enjoy the moral authority, which we habitually associate with states. And in so far as this is true in varying degrees elsewhere, we must reckon this influence as an element, actual or potential, in the parties which englobe and represent these communities. Where such state structures do not survive (appropriately adapted) from pre-colonial times, parties and their leaders may make appeal to the memory of states and leaders, especially if these had a record of "resistance" to the colonial conqueror. So in Guinea, where nothing remains of the state structure of the Mandingo leader Samory Touré, Sékou Touré and his *Parti Démocratique de Guinée* use the memory of his authority to strengthen the loyalty of their own followers. And in a very real sense it is an influence and an inspiration; being still a living tradition, unlike the Brian Borus and Stephen Dushans from which other nationalist movements have drawn encouragement. Guinea is an instructive instance because the P.D.G. is an advanced example of a mass party whose organization and ideology have been heavily influenced from outside.

Another familiar kind of African influence which seems to me to be fairly generally present in the make-up of monopolistic parties is the national sentiment of a dominant people (tribe is too narrow a word in this context). Where the frontiers of a new nation-state coincide with ethnic boundaries this takes place fairly naturally (and the provinces of Nigeria are perhaps state members of a federation for this purpose). But even peoples like the Bakongo, divided between the two Congos and Angola, or the Ewe/Mina divided between Togo and Ghana, or the Mandingo/Bambara people spread through much of western West Africa, make their national sentiment—their awareness of their common language and traditions —felt in the monopolistic parties they dominate, or at least as sectional influences within those parties. It is difficult to think of major parties in modern tropical Africa that are not significantly affected by these sentiments: a fact which might well become more important in the future.

This national sentiment is not the same as the basic Africanness of the parties. This derives from the fact that the societies they represent are African. The mass of the people, who make up the rank and file of such parties, are often only superficially influenced by Western ways. It is true that colonial administration, new methods of production, new economic, political and religious ideas are profoundly modifying and transforming African societies. But only a superficial observer would conclude that the differing and indigenous nature of these societies was disappearing as a result of the transformation. Cultural assimilation of very different societies on a continental scale is a controversial issue. But certainly the time and other necessary conditions have not been present in tropical Africa where cultural assimilation of whole peoples, as opposed to a few individuals, has proved an unsubstantial dream or bogey. The parties are usually all the more mirrors of the peoples they represent because of the close contacts which the party machines maintain with each village or township, usually involving the oral discussion traditional in much of Africa. It has been said with some truth that West Africans are good at politics. This would seem to be partly due at least to the nature of their societies, which have enabled many individuals to participate in political activity: certainly it does not seem to be due to anything imported from outside.

The "African nature" of a political party is not fundamentally less if that party is actively opposed to certain traditional practices and loyalties—determined for instance to break the power of the chiefs and the traditional authorities. The transformation of African societies, the creation of new loyalties and systems, surely remains more of an African issue than the imported formulation of new slogans might suggest. (Marx was far from being a Russian: but it is hard to miss the peculiarly Russian flavour of the Russian Revolution.)

It is important to give due weight in each case to the indigenous influences on African political parties, from pre-colonial state systems to the social and psychological characteristics of African societies. It is equally important to understand the significance of the influences from outside Africa that have gone to mould these parties too.

These influences are considerable in every case. They may be divided into the ideas, techniques and habits instilled by the colonial system itself; and those acquired outside the colonial system, usually from the society of the colonial power.

It would be difficult in a chapter of this length to enumerate the host of ways in which the colonial system has affected African political parties. In the first place the colonial system created the states themselves, the entities which African parties were designed to take over and in most cases now control. There has been singularly little attempt to alter colonial boundaries, though certain small areas have moved across colonial administrative lines. During most of their rather brief period of settled rule these new states were governed autocratically and (broadly speaking) benevolently from outside. A more advanced apparatus of administration was created. The effects of this were tempered in varying degrees by systems of government through, or at least in reliance on, existing local machinery. Colonial rule had a notably greater impact in French territories, where assimilation of one sort or another was the accepted policy and direct rule became increasingly the practice, than in British ones, where in some cases the concept of indirect rule and the separation of black and white people much diminished the effect of the system on the African political parties. In the last period of colonial rule, government increasingly enlisted the participation of the governed: at first in minor administrative positions, and then gradually in political office. In all cases it was this colonial power (which they saw mainly, be it remembered, as autocratic power operating from above rather than elected by any popular

choice between alternatives) that the parties were designed to take over.

A more particular instance of this influence of colonial
policy than what might be called the example of colonial
rule is the precepts advocated for African political life by
the colonial power. Most colonial authorities encouraged
the formation of political parties in the last stages of their
rule, somewhat on the lines of political parties at home,
for participation in local parliamentary assemblies or
indeed in the imperial capital. These parties were intended
by the colonial authorities to be, and often were, rep-
resentative of different groups and opinions within the
colonial community, and ready to co-operate with the
authorities in administering the country. They were intended to have a "democratic" and parliamentary flavour,
often operating within the framework of a limited franchise, rather than para-statal alternatives to colonial rule.
Both in the British and in the French territories, as the
devolution of political power to Africans increased and
the franchise widened, so alternative African parties grew,
often with some official encouragement. A classic example
is the rise in the Gold Coast after the constitutional
advances of 1953 of rival parties to the Convention
People's Party (the London *Times* declared in August
1955 that the vigorous growth of opposition parties constituted "the British Government's greatest dilemma" in
granting independence to the Gold Coast). The growth
of opposition parties designed to protect minority rights
was also a significant phenomenon in the last years of
colonial rule in Northern Rhodesia and Kenya; and
similar tendencies can be seen in most other territories,
for the grip of the para-statal party was rarely strong

enough to crush all opposition. But the fading of these opposition parties after independence seems to me neither remarkable nor tragic. They withered because the conditions which created them—constitutional democracy on the West European pattern and sometimes European support—dried up. And the new African states are less European and more stable as a result.

Even under the French system, where Africans elected representatives to the imperial parliament and were regarded for this purpose as French citizens, we nevertheless find Africans not content for long to vote for the different political parties competing in France. The number of West African deputies to the Assembly was increased in 1946 from the single Senegalese of pre-war times to seventeen. These African deputies soon saw the advantages of collaboration for African purposes across the lines of the French parties which they had joined. By 1948 many of them had organized themselves into two African groups, the *Rassemblement Démocratique Africain* and the *Indépendants d'Outre Mer*. These parties, and especially the R.D.A., grew rapidly into the para-statal mass parties that dominate almost all the French-speaking Republics of West and Equatorial Africa today. The R.D.A. remained for tactical reasons affiliated to the French Communist Party until two years later. After the breach it became more consciously African and held aloof in the French parliament from matters considered purely French.

The precepts advocated for Africans by France and Britain differed in so far as assimilation was never the British intention and there were no African deputies at Westminster. But under the rule of a single mass party the parliamentary forms lose much of their meaning. So long as the parliamentary opposition is negligible or even non-existent, it does not much matter that in former British territories British procedures are followed, while in former French ones the forms are modelled on Paris.

Trade Unions are another form of organization introduced by the colonial authorities into their African territories. From the start the Unions so transplanted acquired political significance and became instruments of African political expression, even if this was not intended by the authorities. The Trade Unions in French territories reflected from the beginning the divisions of the metropolitan Unions; and even after independence these divisions and affiliations to rival groups in France still continue. In British territories Unions were conceived as non-political organizations designed to facilitate industrial bargaining; and they too were patterned after the non-political aspects of the T.U.C., and usually set up and advised by T.U.C. representatives. As soon as the Trade Unions took root in Africa, the same forces began to operate on them as on other forms of political life. In so far as the Unions reflected African aspirations, they always demanded more independence from the colonial power and proclaimed the need for all Trade Union organizations to join hands in order to achieve this. Characteristically the Unions tended to be kept apart by rivalries which are more personal and less deeply ideological than in Europe. African Trade Unionists, especially if involved in other forms of political activity, are indeed also coming increasingly to feel that the experience and advice they received from European Trade Unionists, however genuinely offered, was not really relevant to African problems and to the struggle to independence. It also seemed to the

African leaders that these organizations were being enlisted in international bodies or elsewhere in causes which
were irrelevant, or at any rate marginal to the welfare of
their own members. Against these increasing doubts, the
subsidies, the training, the technical and legal advice, and
the sponsorship in world labour organizations seemed
increasingly less worth having. So it was that in 1957 a
considerable number of the more radical Trade Unionists
in French West and Equatorial Africa set up their own
Union Générale des Travailleurs d'Afrique Noire, with Sékou
Touré of Guinea as its principal animator and formal
insistence on severing affiliation with all non-African
Unions.

Much more significant are the ideas and techniques
learnt by African politicians in Britain or France. Here
again the R.D.A. provides an outstandingly clear example. This party was originally founded by a group of
French black African deputies in Paris in 1948 as a coalition to bring together all the African organizations in
their territories against colonialism. Its leaders, some of
whom were or had been associated with the French Communist Party, quickly saw the advantages of the techniques of organization and party management evolved by
Lenin, and adapted these to their own needs. The with-
drawal from the R.D.A. of those Africans associated with
the French Socialists left the field open to the Communists: who applied themselves vigorously to the task
of helping the party to build up its organization and
encouraging it along paths useful to the world Communist movement. But the Africans, who were glad to
have the French Communists as parliamentary allies, and
to vote with them on non-African issues in return for

Communist votes on African ones, were quick to see and resent any prospect of another group of Frenchmen becoming their masters, or of giving them help in order to use them for non-African ends. Among the various causes of the breach with the Communists led by Houphouet Boigny in 1950, this African suspicion of being used for other ends than their own must rank high. In any case, apart from voting allies in the French parliament, it was not the Communist ideology but the Communist techniques that the R.D.A. leaders wanted to acquire. And this "party technology" they did distinguish from the ideology and adapt to good effect. Some R.D.A. leaders hardly acquired Marxist ways of thought. Even during the period of collaboration with the Communists Houphouet Boigny was prepared to say: "Is it likely that I, Houphouet, a traditional chief, an African doctor, a big landowner and a Catholic, should be a Communist?" But there was a younger and more radical wing of party militants in the R.D.A.; who, while just as African in purpose as their more conservative colleagues, had minds more imbued with Marxist ideology and trained by Marxist habits of thinking. Their influence is clearly visible today in the Guinean and Malian branches of the R.D.A., which now form the dominant single parties in those countries. It is less visible but certainly also present in the other national parties of R.D.A. origin.

We may thus see the new countries of tropical Africa as dominated by these monolithic and all-pervasive political parties; which tended to represent the new independent-state-to-be in embryo even in the last stages of colonial rule, and which now hold the new states together as they grow into nations. Each of these parties derives its authority and its effectiveness in varying degrees both from African traditions and also from techniques and ideologies learnt from the colonial power or from Western civilization in general. These parties can be reckoned as powerful forces for order in the conditions of modern Africa, where the tendencies making for chaos and fragmentation are much stronger than in the more settled polities of the West. Their leadership and party cadres are recruited partly from feudal and traditional ruling groups (less so in former French territories than in former British ones, and to a very varying extent even in ex-British ones); and partly from a new Westernized élite which is often hostile to feudal authorities but indispensable because it alone is capable of running a modern state.

It is superficial to regard these parties as forces for stability only in so far as they are dominated by conservative and feudal elements, and to classify the Western-educated intellectuals as necessarily an influence for disorder, even when they profess rather revolutionary ideologies. On the contrary, there is always the danger that the traditional ruling groups, and the more conservative among the leaders, may attempt to maintain the old ways and certain colonial practices for so long as to provoke a violent reaction,[1] or at least the disaffection of a large proportion of the small educated élite on whom the effective administration of a modern state and modern society must depend. The conservative elements make for stability not automatically, but to the extent that they harness and moderate the evolution from colonial dependency to independent statehood, politically first and then economically and socially. Their most useful contribution

[1] Zanzibar is a good example

to stability is to ease the difficult period of transition. Perhaps more significant is the evidence that the detribalized and Westernized élites, radical though their ideas may be, tend to become a force for stability once their party machine is in control of the government. These leaders and their henchmen have had an essentially "bourgeois" training. They are divorced by a personal gulf unequalled in the West from the peasantry of the African villages and the proletariat of the towns. They, and their wives, have a large personal interest in the power, the position and the standard of living provided by their job in the party or the state. They are basically anxious to lead a Western and middle-class life, and to take the place of the white administrators and experts who have hitherto enjoyed this different and strikingly higher standard. Although the picture sometimes painted by critics of the new independent states, of a small group of African party bosses maintaining themselves in unchallangeable power in an atmosphere of cars, servants and whisky while the masses languish, is an obtuse caricature, it does at least grasp the point that the new party machines are a force for order and stability.

In this connexion it is important to remember that the political leaders of the new states, whether feudal chiefs or detribalized intellectuals, conservatives or radicals, are normally not what for convenience may be called capitalists. That is to say, their power and authority, and the interests of those they represent, do not normally derive from commerce or the direction of private enterprise, or even from the possession of considerable private property as opposed to feudal position. They therefore naturally think of achieving their ends through the exercise of political authority. They have what Mr James Burnham calls managerial values. When they consider consciously what is needed to forge a new nation out of a former colony and how to cause it to develop economically, technically and socially, they do not think of the role of government as being to order and regulate a society whose driving forces come from individuals outside the government structure. They know that in most cases such forces hardly exist. In colonial times economic development and technical and social progress, like government, were in the hands of foreigners, though often of private as opposed to governmental ones. If the new African states now want to do these things, or at least direct them, for themselves, it is through state and party action, or at least state and party stimulus and control, that they think of acting: because outside these organizations the native motives and skills are not there. What underlies ideas of African Socialism, of Sékou Touré's "la primauté de la politique" and of Nkrumah's "seek ye first the political kingdom", is this need for the state to provide the main motive force in economic and social development, whatever the position assigned to foreign and even indigenous aid and enterprise within a system of political control, as much as the obvious point that political independence must come first. It seems fair to say that African society, and more particularly the party leaderships, are so constituted that there is a fundamental pull towards the state (in double harness with the party which functions as a para-state) as the natural and indeed the only effective instrument of advance. The implications of this are reflected in subsequent chapters of this book.

Chapter Four

TECHNICAL DEFICIENCIES

THE new societies of tropical Africa, and especially their ruling élites, are on the whole good at political organization. So long as the dominant issue in a territory was the attainment of independence, the efforts and attention of politically conscious Africans were concentrated on this goal. But now that European political authority has come to an end, and Africans have assumed the responsibilities of government, they are becoming increasingly concerned with the technical and economic problems which confront them in their effort to become modern nation-states.

The process of transition from the traditional societies of Africa into the modern world began in the period before colonialism. It is not necessary to trace here the transmission of Mediterranean civilization and techniques to tropical Africa by Islamic and even earlier agencies. After the Age of Discovery in the fifteenth century precolonial contacts between tropical Africa and the developing countries of Western Europe (themselves also the pupils of Mediterranean civilization) gradually increased. The African cultural tradition was able, on the whole, to assimilate what it learnt in this way. The really kinetic and overwhelming impact of the West on Africa dates from the industrial and technical revolution which Europe began to export to Africa seriously in the colonial era.

Now the newly independent states must take this process a stage further—for there is no going back—and at the same time adapt it more directly to the needs of their own societies. And in doing so they find themselves obliged to pay much more attention than before to the intractable problems of technological advance.

Technological progress confronts the newly independent countries of tropical Africa with three main problems. Firstly, independence itself, even where is it conceded without undue struggle, creates what has been called a revolution of rising expectations in the new countries. Both leaders and followers want a faster rate of advance than before. But secondly, the technological gap between these new countries and the most advanced societies is immense, and steadily increasing. Thirdly, the impact of the modern world is destroying the fabric of traditional society faster than it creates, in the ways and minds of men in the less-advanced countries, a new social fabric adapted to modern technological life.

All these aspects of technological change in Africa are worth examining. And all of them depend for their eventual resolution on greatly increased education and technical training: much of which must be imported from outside.

The impact of the technically advanced countries on the more backward ones is everywhere great and immediately visible. Areas which were under colonial administration appear to have usually been transformed more than others. To those who believed in material progress it was reassuring to see these backward lands "catching up", developed by the engineering, medical and other technical skills brought into them. But many Africans and others thought that under colonialism these improvements did not accrue as much as they might have to the local inhabitants, or at any rate to most of them. The language of anti-colonialism was picturesque and emotionally satisfying. To quote the President of Indonesia for example: "From our experience of colonialism we know how wealth ... was drawn off into the cooking pots of Europe's commercial and industrial kitchens. For centuries the wealth of Asia, Africa and Latin America was sucked up by the colonial powers of Europe. Our people bear the marks of suffering and degradation brought about through the drawing off of untold wealth."[1] The charges of exploitation were believed by many and seemed particularly true of the areas that had made the greatest material advance, the areas of white settlement. There the rest of the population was relegated to a helot status, whether they were present before the arrival of the European colonizers or came or were brought in afterwards. Was it not logical to assume that the end of colonial rule and of European privilege would enable the benefits of technological progress to be more fairly and widely distributed?

This at least was the message which the outside world expounded to the African élites, in the circles they frequented and the books and newspapers they read, both in the imperial countries themselves and even more insistently in America and the Communist countries. Not only were national liberty and political independence the birthright of all peoples. They brought with them higher standards of living. And the élites used the whole machinery of the mass political parties and other forms of anti-

[1] I presume it is not necessary to explain how far from the complex economic realities this rhetoric is.

colonial agitation to pass on this message of greater wealth after freedom to the rest of the population. The future rulers of the new states have encouraged their followers to expect a faster rate of material and social betterment just at the time when their own take-over from the more competent European authorities makes it difficult to maintain even the standards that prevailed under colonial rule.

The assumption that colonial rule held back technical progress was fostered by certain Marxists with their analytical theory of imperialism as the final and most exploitative phase of capitalism. It was also encouraged by progressive Western liberals with their more generous desire to establish human equality and dignity. Both held that colonialism was the essential cause of the misfortunes and the relative backwardness of tropical Africa. Both Marxists and progressive liberals implied that progress and national development—the growth of a society at once richer and better adjusted to the modern world—would follow naturally once the artificial restraints of alien domination were removed.

In fact, as we have seen, the colonial system did distort the progress of tropical Africa towards modern statehood. In some ways this distortion has turned out to be greater than the colonial authorities themselves realized. But colonial rule has at the same time been the main agency of this progress; and on balance the distortions it caused are more due to lopsided development than to actual inhibition. The pathetic inadequacy of the belief that the mere removal of colonial rule would in itself provide a solution to the problem of technological backwardness has been brought home to both Africans and others by the coming of independence to most of the former colonial empires.

The American scholar Lucian Pye, writing of the hope that the new countries faced with these problems might also become political democracies into the bargain, ruefully observes that: "As Americans, we believed we had a complete policy in our anti-colonial tradition, for we assumed once a people had independence, they would inevitably and spontaneously move towards democracy. This romantic and anti-intellectual view of national development had tended to deter us from hard, rational analysis of the problem of nation-building." Many British sympathizers with the cause of African freedom will recognize themselves in this passage.

As the African political leaders approached positions of political responsibility most of them seem to have become increasingly conscious that, unjust and humiliating as colonial rule might be, it was not the root cause of African technical backwardness. They and those of their followers who are animated at least partly by national idealism and not purely by selfishness realize that what they dream of for their countries are everyday advantages in the more advanced societies they have seen. They are aware that after independence it is "almost impossible to obtain from within their own meagre economies the wherewithal to support even the level of public services they were accustomed to during the colonial era". They must continue to get help from outside: if possible more help than before. Some of them see that not all the help they are likely to get will be enough for their purposes.

It is at this point that a new and disturbing prospect has begun to open up before the African leaders in the domain of technological advance. They see the evidence that the gap between the most scientifically and socially advanced communities and the more backward ones, far from diminishing, is in fact steadily growing. Some two hundred years ago, before the industrial and technical revolution began in earnest, the difference between a man's capacities in different parts of the world was not so great as it is today. Napoleon, it has been pointed out, could take an army across the Alps hardly any more quickly or efficiently than Hannibal. Since then the pace of technical advance in the more advanced communities has been steadily increasing. Africans in advanced countries see that these developments in technology have transformed the structure of society there. "Unskilled" labour and the ignorance and poverty which went with it were until recently the lot of most people even in what were then advanced societies. Though agriculture and a range of crafts were practised with traditional knowledge and skill, as in Africa today, they were not productive enough to yield much material wealth. Modern technology has made possible a society with less craftsmanship perhaps, but so much greater productivity that a fuller, richer and more equalitarian life becomes possible for almost everybody.

Habits of thought are changing too. Instead of handing down and slowly modifying a stock of traditional wisdom infused with religious beliefs and political precedents, men in advanced countries tend increasingly to accept as certain only what can be demonstrated by objective experiment; and to judge religious, political and other traditions by what seem to be their material results, treating them as man-made and imperfect expedients for ordering society which can, like mechanical processes, be radically changed in response to the advances of science and technology.

Educated Africans are aware, of course, that inevitably much of this technical know-how generated in the West, and the social possibilities it carries with it, have spilt over into the areas which are not generating these changes. As areas like North America and Russia come to equal or surpass Western Europe in technology, its effects are still more widely disseminated. But Africans also see that this overspill into less-developed areas does not proceed so fast as technological progress in the advanced societies themselves.

And so all the time the difference is growing between the technical achievements of the advanced countries and the backward ones, and between the material and social advantages which the two different types of community in practice provide for themselves. And the argument that the developed world has so far introduced these technological advances into the more backward areas of the world largely by its own exertions and for its own benefit only emphasizes the extent and nature of the gap.

The technical revolution in the more advanced countries also carries with it other difficulties for less-developed tropical areas. As science increases the gap between what can be achieved in an advanced society and a backward one, it becomes more profitable for the advanced countries to reinvest inside their own economies the resources they produce. The chance of greater gain, which drew private capital and enterprise from Europe into the more primitive economies of tropical Africa, is diminishing. At the same time technological progress threatens the position in the advanced economies of those commodities in which tropical countries have specialized. New discoveries have made most of them easier to produce. Agricultural techniques have greatly improved, and new areas have been brought into production. Many of the staple commodities, both temperate and tropical, look like being in more or less permanent surplus in the Western world. Cotton and coffee, on which many tropical countries now depend almost entirely for their economic relations with the outside world, are only the most conspicuous examples of an increasing problem. And the position is made still worse for the tropical countries which relied on these staple commodities by the resourcefulness of modern technology. Substitutes and alternatives are continually being discovered for a growing list of tropical products; and it is becoming increasingly expedient, for economic or political reasons, to produce these alternatives at home.[1]

A further source of concern is that the widening tech-

---

[1] One great asset which tropical Africa possesses is its wild life. The wild animals and birds of Africa are the most spectacular of any continent, and many of them are alas already rather rare. Hitherto most Africans have tended to regard wild animals as their enemies, as threats either directly to themselves or to their livestock and their crops; while other Africans have regarded certain species as valuable sources of food or income. The preservation of wild life in game reserves and by other means has hitherto been almost entirely the work of colonial authorities, and has usually been unpopular. But the new African governments, taking stock of such resources as they can muster and anxious to take their place in the community of civilized states, are beginning to realise the great importance of their wild animals and birds as tourist attractions. There is no doubt about the wealth which the great and rapidly growing tourist industry can bring to any country with real attractions to offer. Wild life in Africa, in scenery which is often itself spectacular, has a deeply moving effect on almost all visitors. If adequate facilities are provided, Africa's fauna can become a considerable source both of revenue from outside and of national pride.

nological gap makes it harder for the developing countries to diversify their own economies by industrializing efficiently. The machinery required is continually becoming more complex. It costs more to buy, and needs more skill to operate and to maintain. Inefficiency and mishandling nowadays send up costs alarmingly. And cheap unskilled labour, with which most underdeveloped countries have hoped to make up the balance, tends to play an ever smaller part. The introduction of advanced industrial plant tends to require less labour than before, but needs that labour to be more skilled. And though the introduction of such plant into tropical African countries may enrich and strengthen its economy in other ways, it no longer distributes wealth widely by hiring a large labour force.

One striking illustration of these difficulties, among many which might be chosen, is provided by African airlines. An airline owned and operated by an African country has prestige value and other important advantages. But it is not easy to operate such an airline without serious loss. Modern jet aircraft cost a great deal of money to buy and to maintain, as do the foreign technicians who fly and service them. Even if the aircraft can be kept in the air, there may not be enough traffic to justify doing so. The same can prove true of oil refineries and other modern industrial plant which the new countries want for reasons that are not exclusively economic. It is true that such advanced industrial enterprises bring important gains in the technical training and the diversification of the economy. But even so the technological gap continues in most cases to widen.

The third problem of technological advance is how to

create in Africa a society capable of supporting it. Modern civilization requires a community in which most of the citizens can for example read and follow written directions, maintain simple equipment like a bicycle or a gas cooker, and know enough about hygiene, diet and medicine to make fairly sensible personal choices among the immense range of foods and drugs individually offered in place of the traditional tribal wisdom. But these abilities are not just skills to be learnt by themselves. They require a new organization of society and a new attitude of mind. Industrialization, says Mr Guy Hunter, is "not simply a combination of scientific knowledge and applied techniques but the motives and values of a society which has the will to use and develop this knowledge and whose institutions reflect and support this system of values".

No independent tropical African country had yet established such a society. Many Africans, still encompassed by the traditional ways of life, are hardly aware of any problem. Things like money and radios and new methods of agriculture come their way gradually without disturbing the old standards and values overmuch. But many more now find the old ways inadequate as guides to conduct in the new world into which they have been drawn. At times the traditional codes seem even to make things more difficult. How many Africans today chafe under the need to support distant relatives from their pitifully insufficient earnings? Yet the new world is not yet theirs either. They are in a condition of flux between the two. This new world is something alien: something that must be consciously acquired and learnt, like its European languages and the use of its machines. That is one of the compulsive forces behind the hunger for education which so impresses visitors to modern Africa. Education is the highway into the modern world, away from the bush and the tribal traditions.

The more thoughtful and sophisticated leaders of the new African states are all too painfully familiar with the problems which perplex their countrymen in the no-man's-land between the old ways and the new. Most of them have passed through it themselves. And they understand the eagerness for education. Not only was it their own way forward; they recognize that education on a still much wider scale is the essential means of creating a new and modern society. It is not only a question of what can be taught in school. The need is to disseminate throughout Africa the whole range of skills familiar in the more advanced countries. And it is obvious to Africans that they cannot do this by themselves.

But while the need for education in this widest sense is plain enough, it is much more difficult for the African leaders to see what a modern African society should be like. In colonial times their criterion was naturally the society of the imperial power. Certain aspects were to be copied, others rejected. But as the responsibilities of independence settle down on the shoulders of the African leaders, and as they come to grapple with the very different problems of their own country, the imperial power becomes less relevant as a general frame of reference.

To begin with, the more thoughtful Africans see that, like every other aspect of the technological revolution, the societies of the developed countries are changing and adapting themselves faster than the backward ones, and too fast to serve as useful static models. As with science, so with society: the gap is getting wider. In one sense this is a daunting prospect. But it also suggests to the shrewder Africans that it would be foolish to set themselves to copy laboriously the present pattern of society and institutions in England or France. This pattern will soon be hopelessly out of date. Nor are Western, and especially English and French, models the only relevant ones. President Senghor of Senegal, to take an outstanding case, is a man imbued with French culture and a significant contributor to it. It might be supposed that he would be content with France as his exemplar, and so in the main he and those who think like him doubtless are. But he sees the objective need, and senses the desire of younger Senegalese, to look beyond France: not just to the traditions of tribal Senegal and of Islam, but to the wide world beyond. In particular, a new and technically very competent society seems to have evolved in the Communist world since Lenin shut the window which Peter the Great had opened on the West. Few Africans want to copy this model either. The conclusion they draw is that the technology is much the same everywhere, and must be learnt; but the social structure can vary.

This conclusion is strengthened by the instinct of national pride and the sense of being African, which leads to the desire to find African solutions to the problems of society and the institutions of the state. Moreover, current trends in the social sciences—history, sociology and anthropology—also suggest that in any case the various ways in which other societies adapt themselves to modern technology are not so directly relevant to the problems of Africa as had been tacitly assumed. No one culture, neither the West nor Communism, can produce a universal pattern of social organization. It is coming to be a truism in the newly independent countries to declare that an advanced African society ought to be, and will be, something different. And if the present pattern of other societies seems less relevant than before, the past stages of their evolution seem less relevant still. Scarcely any African leader believes that his country and his continent need to pass through the experience of the European nineteenth century in order to arrive at an African twentieth-century answer.

The form which their new societies will take is therefore difficult for Africans to foresee. The technological revolution is moving so fast that it will confront them with quite unexpected opportunities and difficulties. West Africans at least feel some confidence—and legitimately—in their political ability; and they expect their new social patterns to grow at least partly round the political institutions described in Chapter Three. The influence of the West, which not only evolved modern technology but imported it directly and forcibly into Africa, will also remain very great.

It seems to me that many Africans, in the emotional relief of independence and in their awareness that the former colonial power is not a model to be patiently aped, underestimate the major role which the West must play in shaping the new Africa. Those who see these problems are themselves a Westernized élite. The impact of the modern world has so far come to their countries through colonialism from the West. And the West is likely to supply the major part of the outside aid and expertise which the new countries will need to carry the transition successfully forward. In the former French territories the scale of French aid will probably ensure that for some years the main source of inspiration will be France. In the former British and Belgian territories the sources will in most cases be equally Western, but drawn more eclectically from the West as a whole. And in all the new African countries, what is learnt from outside will become more purely technical, as distinctive African forms of society begin to reassert themselves after the removal of alien colonial authority.

Chapter Five

ECONOMICS, AID AND THE PRIMACY
OF POLITICS

WE have seen that the new African countries have
shown themselves able at politics, and have established successful systems of government, usually of a
somewhat authoritarian kind. We have also seen that they
inherited from colonial times lopsidedly developed and
even artificial or greenhouse economies, suitable for out-
lying provinces of a trading empire, but ill adapted to
independence; and that they now find themselves con-
fronted with the stubborn realities of technological backwardness as well, It is therefore not surprising, indeed it is
to be expected, that when they turn their attention to
these economic and technical problems they see them
largely in the political terms they understand, and seek
largely political solutions.

These problems did not seem so great to Africans in
colonial times as they do now. As the excitement of independence wanes, they obtrude themselves ever more
insistently on men hitherto unused to thinking about
them and ill prepared to deal with them. Indeed in the
new states economic and technical difficulties often become so serious that the attempts to solve them play
a major part in shaping the whole process of nation-
building.

The logic, one might say the momentum, of decolonization is that it should extend from the political to the
economic sphere. This does not mean that the new states

should cut themselves off from the profitable commerce with Europe that pre-colonial African polities so eagerly sought. But it does mean that they want to be masters in their own house economically as well as politically, and able to deal with their former colonial masters and other outside powers in their own interests as they conceive them. This is a general desire, which animates both moderates and radicals. You were the first, said the moderate President Senghor in his eulogy of the equally moderate President Tubman during the Liberian state visit to Senegal of 1962, to see and to proclaim to the rest of us that political independence is a hollow vessel unless it is completed by economic independence too.[1]

Economic independence is a self-evident concept. But how to achieve it in practice is less easy to define with any precision. Different groups of leaders in Africa, faced with broadly similar problems, have made very different decisions about how to deal with them. The ultimate goals are doubtless broadly the same. But there are many ways of getting there; and these ways appeal to Africans for different political reasons. In the new Africa the economic realities do not determine the nature of political action. Rather, the solutions adopted for economic problems are essentially a matter of political choice. And they need to be examined in a political context.

Externally the essence of the economic problem is how to obtain from abroad, and especially from the most advanced countries, the products and skills which Africa needs—and now needs more than ever, as the economy requires to be brought into balance, as the technological gap widens and as expectations grow. Only a portion of

[1] Quoted from memory

these products and skills can be bought and paid for at the market price. What should a new African country buy in this way? How, and where, and on what terms should it try to procure the balance? What proportion of this balance should it forgo in order to preserve or extend its independence? These are political decisions that will determine in each African state the complex pattern of trade and aid.

Internally the issue is to decide the goals of economic activity, and the extent of governmental coercion in pursuit of these goals. For the African societies that are now struggling to make themselves into viable states all suffer from a serious scarcity of almost every economic resource and skill, both imported and locally produced. In some favoured countries these shortages may be somewhat less than others. But none of them is in a position to remedy these shortages in the near future; and in the poorest the deficiencies are so great as to make one despair of their ever becoming viable states, able to pay their own way by producing the equivalent of what they consume. A state faced with this long-term scarcity of almost every resource must decide how far to control and plan its economy. The degree to which it does so, the priorities it elects to lay down about the use of these resources, are not mere matters of expediency or of economic determinism. They are fundamental decisions about how to build a new nation. They affect the ultimate purposes of society. And so internally too the choice of methods presents itself to Africans as a political issue.

The political nature of these decisions is obscured by the general tendency of radicals and advocates of state control, in Africa and elsewhere, to proclaim that their political purpose is the direction of economic life, whereas conservatives and believers in economic *laisser-faire* tend to say that they oppose political interference in the free development of the economy. But of course in the new countries of Africa, whose economies have hitherto been developed from the outside, the first question to arise is how far the economic pattern inherited from colonial times should be changed at all. Whatever the answer to this question may be, in any given state it is a political one. President M'Ba of Gabon, for instance, decided to leave things very much as they were, at least for a time. This decision was based on Monsieur M'Ba's political judgement about how best to obtain the benefits he most values for his country and its people. President Sékou Touré of Guinea, faced with much the same decisions, for equally political reasons chose a radical breach. In former British West Africa, the economic policies of Nigeria and Ghana show a similar but milder divergence.

When therefore the radical African leaders proclaim the political nature of the economic and technical decisions they and other African governments take, it seems to me they have a valid point. President Sékou Touré's "la primauté de la politique", and President Nkrumah's biblical "seek ye first the political kingdom", have as their first and most obvious meaning that the way economic problems are tackled depends on who has the political authority. But the primacy of politics in modern Africa has a deeper meaning than that.

Let us take the external aspect first. The general desire in Africa for political independence carries with it as a natural corollary the desire to end "economic colonialism" too. The aspiration and the ultimate intention seem to me to be always there. It is in the speed of the advance, and the methods of getting there, that the variation comes. Economic independence may not always seem very expedient as an immediate objective. The economic loss of a very abrupt break can far outweigh the gain. Even the radical governments of tropical Africa have in fact proceeded more cautiously than their words suggest. Both Ghana and Mali have been careful to preserve many of the traditional ties of aid and trade with the former colonial power; and Guinea's decision to go it alone was at least as much due to the French Government's refusal to continue massive aid to a country that had voted to leave the Community as to Guinean dislike of such links.

The issue of economic independence, and of how fast it is being achieved, is thus a crucial political issue in Africa, and one on which those in positions of authority in the new countries are particularly sensitive. They look closely at the pattern of economic relationships, and the nature and extent of the aid, that bind them and their neighbours to their former colonial masters. In so far as the same economic pattern continues as before the handover of political power, in so far as commercial activity is still mainly concerned with producing one or two particular commodities for distant markets at prices which the new government is unable to control, in so far as the country seems no nearer to paying its own way, so they feel that in spite of the achievement of political independence "economic colonialism" still continues. And Africans know that the pace of advance is not conditioned by the natural resources and trained manpower available: there are rich and poor countries among the hustlers, and among the cautious. On the contrary, the speed of advance, and the sacrifices made to attain it, seem to depend on the political inclinations of the ruling group, and especially of the leader.

Certainly not all African leaders today regard economic colonialism, or moving away from it only at a snail's pace, as the greatest evil. Many of them already see very clearly, and more are coming to realize, that the central problem for all underdeveloped states, whether emerging from colonial rule or not, is how to obtain the vast range of goods and services, the capital and the technical skill that they need in order to develop. The most satisfactory way of obtaining these things is to be in a position to pay for them by exporting commodities that the rest of the world is willing to pay for. A sheltered market for a crop, or for a mineral already in production, therefore is not something to be lightly discarded; even though the price may fluctuate and even though certain economic and other servitudes have to be accepted in return.

Nevertheless, every African leader is himself responsive in some degree to the great political longing for independence; and the most active and useful of his followers are likely to feel this even more strongly. The problem cannot therefore be limited to determining how to continue most profitably after independence the colonial economic process of producing specialized commodities for assured markets. African leaders must also decide how, and how fast, they propose to work towards an economic independence corresponding to their newly won political freedom. They all want to produce a more balanced economy and eventually to stand on their own in the world, free from the servitude which economic colonialism entails. Some leaders are anxious not to endanger in the process such prosperity and such social improvement as may be attainable; and for this reason they are willing to proceed slowly. Others feel justified in making the community, or at least certain sections of it, forgo some short-term economic advantage, both in order to attain political ends and in order to put the economy on a solider footing for the future. But these are questions of means towards what is essentially the same goal.

The most obvious way to lessen your economic dependence on one country, or on one export crop, is to diversify. And diversification in various forms is therefore the usual policy of the new African governments. First there must be diversification of the sources of supply; away from the exclusive reliance on the former metropolitan power and its economy, towards other purveyors of the many things which Africans need to import. Secondly there must be diversification of production, so that a wider range of goods (especially foodstuffs) is produced at home, and so that the country becomes less dependent on the export of one or two products. This may in time lead, it is hoped, to the third form of diversification, that of markets. If your exports are not limited to a single and perhaps artificial market, your dependence on the power that provides it is greatly lessened.

African governments tend to put the diversification of the sources of supply first, both because it is easier to achieve than producing a wider range of goods, and because it carries with it a greater feeling of political independence. In the British and Belgian territories, indeed, this diversification of the sources of consumer and even capital goods was largely the rule in colonial times. The Congo Basin Treaties guaranteed an open door commercial system over a sizeable proportion of all tropical Africa, and made such devices as Imperial Preference impossible. And outside this area the aid given by the British Government to its colonial territories under the Colonial Development and Welfare system, for instance, was in no way tied to British exports, and was much criticised by interested manufacturers precisely for this reason. But for the governments of the new countries it is not merely a question of whether private traders and contractors in the country are able to buy their imports from any source according to value. The desire for diversification among African nationalists means a wish to emancipate their countries' economies from the very substantial economic connexion with the imperial system to which they formerly belonged, and which the trade statistics reflect even in the most liberal colonial administrations; and also to obtain technical and administrative advice from sources other than the former administering power, if only as a check on the advice given them by their former masters.

As the new governments struggle in this way to modify and broaden their economic relationship with the outside world, they do not make the clear distinction between trade and aid, between commerce and charity, that is present in the minds of Westerners. Fortunately for the new countries, many of the things they need from outside —the goods, the facilities, the expertise—can be obtained in the modern world without paying the full market price for them. Sometimes they are available as gifts. But over the years a whole range of modifications of the market price has been worked out; and these modifications, though falling short of outright gifts, mitigate the cost to the underdeveloped economy. At one end of the scale are technical devices like reduced rates of interest, deferred payment, generous credit, and guarantees by the government of the advanced country to its traders against default. More specific elements of aid in commerce with underdeveloped countries include guaranteed markets and prices for exports, sometimes involving agreements to buy above the world market price—a device which sustains the economies of most of the former French African territories. At the other end of the scale, most of the technical material and expertise received by the new African countries in the social, medical, military and educational fields, for instance, contains a large element of gift. No African country pays in full for the imported equipment, the imported experts and the training of its own nationals for its armed forces, its hospitals and dispensaries, and its schools.

These calculations of where the balance of economic and political advantage lies, always remembering that an extra discount on one transaction may upset another donor and lead to losses elsewhere, apply directly to imports on government account and to semi-governmental schemes like the Volta project in Ghana. Ordinary commercial trading is usually controlled and shepherded by indirect means, and within certain limits is sometimes still left free. Most African states still allow the importation by private traders of a substantial range of consumer goods, replacements for machinery and other "maintenance imports". In colonial times a large part of these imports came from the metropolitan power, or at least from other units of the imperial system. This privileged position for the goods of the colonial power was maintained in a variety of ways, from open arrangements like tariff preference to more discreet methods. It was most effective in the French colonies. Today the governments of almost all the former French territories still restrict the bulk of their commercial imports to the franc zone, for which their currencies can be freely used. A system of agreed exchange control between these countries and France strictly fixes and rations imports from outside the franc zone, by allocating specific quantities of non-franc currencies for purchases which are defined in some detail. Each French African country normally receives a global amount of such currencies in excess of the foreign currency earned by its exports outside the franc zone. In other African countries importers are usually allowed more latitude of choice within the limits set by the government for private trade. But here too tariffs, quotas and other devices may deter imports of certain goods, and favour those which the government considers helpful to its development plans—in other words, politically desirable.

In all this field of trade-and-aid the African governments are well aware of the spirit of competition and rivalry between the donor powers. This is not only a manifestation of the cold war, though the rivalry between the Western and Eastern blocs is particularly clear. Between the Western powers there is the element of commercial competition. And the former colonial powers are sometimes jealous about aid even by their friends to the countries they once administered (a feeling stronger in the case of some ex-colonial powers than others). The revival of this competition is one aspect of the general reversion of Africa's relations with the outside world to the pattern which prevailed before the colonial partition.

It helps to ensure that Africans obtain some of the goods and services they need more cheaply than they otherwise might, even when they continue to obtain them almost exclusively from one source. It is therefore not unwelcome to Africans on purely financial grounds, quite apart from the political advantages it brings them.

The competition between the richer powers does not of course by itself explain why they give the aid they do. In fact these gifts and concessions, these mitigations of the full vigour of the market rate, are made by donors for a variety of reasons: each of which influences some donors and some types of aid more than others. These motives for giving aid have often been described. They are worth listing here because they represent what the donor sees as his advantage in the bargains struck with African recipients, and because the recognition of them helps to make the business of aid more understandable to Africans too.

First there is missionary zeal. It moves not only religious bodies, but also those who wish to see the principles they hold dear practised as widely as possible. Much of the aid offered to Africa is at least partly influenced by the desire to see a certain political system established in the recipient country: whether this is parliamentary democracy, communism or some other form of government.

Secondly, there is the acceptance of responsibility, which the well-to-do in a modern society feel towards the less privileged. In advanced countries there is general approval of social services supported by differential taxation, and of other aid by the state and by corporate bodies. In such countries the area of governmental responsibility has been extended to ensure minimum levels of welfare for all the citizens. This responsibility was further enlarged in the later years of colonialism to include some effort to raise the far lower standards of social welfare in the dependencies administered by imperial governments. Once this human need was acknowledged, the sense of obligation to help alleviate it did not disappear with the granting of political independence. So aid by the metropolitan power after independence has continued, notably in the field of education: and most conspicuously in the case of France.

A third reason for aid by the former metropolitan power is to preserve the ties which formerly linked it to its overseas possessions in Africa. The main element here is commercial. The trade of the new countries was in colonial times largely conducted by citizens of the administering power; and the desire to protect and develop this trade was as we have seen one of the main reasons for the establishment of colonial authority in the nineteenth century. This economic activity, in both directions, has by now often come to represent a sizeable investment by the colonizing economy; and it is natural for the government of a former colonial power to try to protect this investment and this trade by offering inducements to the newly independent countries. These inducements affect the terms of the trade itself (quotas, tariff preferences, subsidies, etc.), and also include other offers likely to influence African governments in some need of aid. At the same time, now that conditions of trade are reverting towards those which prevailed before the era of colonial exclusiveness, other countries also see it as legitimate to offer advantages designed among other things to help their trade. A familiar example of this is the tied loan or gift, which must be spent within the economy of the donor country.

Military and strategic advantage is a parallel and equally understandable concern of donor governments. In colonial times the overseas territories of an imperial nation were a major extension of its power—in controlled resources, in strategic strongpoints, and sometimes in manpower. Many colonies were annexed for strategic reasons, or grew from naval or military bases. These considerations weigh much less heavily with the ex-imperial countries in the changed circumstances of today than they formerly did; and certainly less than is sometimes alleged. Whether the overseas bases, the manpower, or even the control of resources like iron ore and oil still have any great value at all in tropical Africa, is a much argued issue. But in so far as governments think it is, or may be, important to retain some measure of control over these assets, or at least to keep them out of hostile hands, they will naturally offer inducements to the new countries concerned to agree. Similarly other powers will try to procure such strategic advantages as they think worth competing for. A common and direct inducement in this field is military aid—the offer to train and equip the small armies of the new African powers free of charge or at reduced prices. But almost any form of aid or "commercial generosity" may have some flavour of strategic purpose, among other motives.

Cultural considerations also play their part. In the main they correspond to commercial and strategic ones, though they may seem sometimes to have an almost missionary flavour about them. Many ex-imperial powers which have quite renounced any idea of political suzerainty over a country formerly administered by them nevertheless remain very anxious to preserve the use of their language, their educational traditions and other cultural links. French governments in particular have traditionally attached great importance to the *rayonnement de la culture française*, and devote very large sums of money and numbers of able men to spreading and maintaining it. The benefit to those who learn is as clear as the benefit to the French taxpayer. Other governments do less in this field. But all former colonial powers make efforts to keep alive their language and culture in areas they have administered; and for a variety of reasons many other governments also try to spread at least some knowledge of their cultural achievements. It is not uncommon to meet Africans who have been taught Bulgarian, Hebrew, Swedish, Chinese or some other language at the expense of a foreign government or institution.

Some observers also see in the dispensing of aid the influence of less tangible factors. These include a sense of guilt and the wish to atone; a desire for international respectability or feelings of *noblesse oblige*; a sense of pride; and a half-stated fear of mounting hostility between rich and poor communities if standards of welfare are allowed to diverge too sharply in an age of rising expectations.

It is not easy to assess the weight of each of these motives in the minds of the various governments, foundations and other organizations when they offer a particular rate of interest or scholarship. But the cold war and the underlying fear of "neo-colonialism" are always there ready to remind the recipients of the less noble of these motives. Africans naturally see the outside world as spinning a complicated web of advantages in their relations with the new countries, in which the actual commercial value of any one transaction only plays a limited part. The decisive factors, it seems to many Africans, are political. And so they too, in deciding what aid to accept, what commitments to incur, what and where to buy and sell, feel that they must likewise be guided by political considerations. This is the second meaning of the slogan: *la primauté de la politique*.

The same sense that decisions are essentially political is also clearly visible internally in the approach of the new African governments—and indeed those of underdeveloped countries generally—to the diversification and industrialization of their own economies. The basic decision to diversity is itself a political one, as we have seen. It stems from the desire for economic decolonization, and especially the sense that this involves emancipation from dependence on one or two export products. Planning experts legitimately point out that it is often in the strict sense "uneconomic" to produce for local consumption a wider range of foodstuffs and other necessities like sugar which the imperial authorities may have discouraged. But this cannot be the decisive argument. Indeed the experts seconded to African governments rarely lay undue emphasis on these international concepts. They are aware that politics must be trumps. And it is difficult to calculate the purely economic factors. Both land and agricultural manpower are underemployed in most African countries. Resources applied to diversifying and increasing agricultural output for local consumption are only marginally diverted from other production. There is plenty of room for improving the quantity and quality of export crops as well, in so far as this is worth while in a world dominated by quotas and sheltered markets, and always on the verge of export surpluses of tropical products. In any case the demands on foreign exchange, to procure all the goods and services from abroad that Africans at this stage of development simply cannot produce adequately themselves, are so great that anything which can be produced at home, even if it is rather inferior and costs rather more effort than the imported product, at least makes it possible for something more essential to be bought abroad.

The complexity of these problems, and the need of the new governments to husband, ration and direct their slender resources if they are to achieve any degree of material progress and economic decolonization, has led all of them to adopt some degree of general economic planning. In this they are encouraged by the tendency in this direction in the more advanced economies. But their needs are clearly greater. And the administrative background of the African élite of today enables it to understand the implementation of a plan better than it does the operations of a free market which is almost entirely outside African control or competence. Plans for diversification and development are therefore now an accepted feature of African government.

The major political decision which confronts the new states of tropical Africa when attempting to plan the diversification of their economies is the degree of governmental control to employ. This issue of the amount of state control and even state ownership of those features of economic life which are essential for development affects not only the nature of society but also the attitude of the outside world, and particularly private capital. Here two factors confront the African policymakers. The first is ideology. Some African parties and their leaders are wedded to African Socialism or even to variants of Marxism as a matter of political belief; and they will be inclined to carry the process of state control and ownership as far as the economic realities of the situation will allow. Others believe more specifically in a liberal economy, either for its own sake or partly at least because this seems the best way of ensuring a maximum of outside aid and investment. The second factor is the economic realities of the situation, both internal and external.

One striking feature of the colonial economy inherited by the new African countries is the almost total lack of native capital. Even ordinary wholesale trade is largely in non-African hands, although those who conduct it may sometimes have been born in the African country concerned. And certainly all large-scale capital investment, whether in mining, manufacturing or extensive plantations, is financed by what since independence has become foreign capital. How far, Africans tend to ask themselves, can a country be economically independent and sovereign if the commanding positions in the economy are controlled by foreigners? The virtual absence of African capital makes even those who incline to a free and capitalist economy and private enterprise think in terms of governmental planning and control, and what is sometimes called state capitalism or governmental investment in partnership with private capital. Others of a more socialist bent draw more radical conclusions.

The general scarcity of resources is another compelling argument in favour of the establishment of priorities and the firm allocation of the means needed to achieve them, if diversification and development are to be realized. Many of the new states are disappointingly poor in mineral wealth; and much of tropical Africa is relatively unsuitable for agriculture. Against this background the unsatisfied demand for consumer goods and improved social services, the rising expectations of rich and poor, Westernized and non-Westernized Africans, is so insistent that only a strong government can divert local resources and foreign imports away from consumption towards the broadening and development of the economy. This is what may be called the development aspect of the general need for strong government in the new nation-states of Africa. But it reinforces the tendency towards state capitalism or socialism, and away from reliance on private enterprise to produce the economic development required.

Another—some would say the main—factor which influences the educated African élites in favour of a high degree of governmental control of the economy is that most of these élites have been trained for administration rather than for business. Politics and government service have been the main channels of advancement; with the law, education and other professions apt to offer better prospects than commerce or banking. Many of the ablest men in French Africa were deputies or Ministers in Paris; and their equivalents in British territories often saw the modern world from a government office. Added to this background there is now the pervasive influence of the all-embracing party, which thinks in political terms and seeks to use the state as its instrument. Government control of economic life is a means of party control—that control which even in the para-statal days before independence the party tried to establish over every aspect of

African public life, including the economic. Both the individual training of leading Africans and the structure of political life incline the new states towards a directed economy, and away from free and foreign-managed enterprise.

Because these pressures towards governmental control and planning are political in origin and have political objectives, the feasibility of a plan in the first place and its success when put into force must be measured by the extent to which it achieves these objectives. Some government plans are ably and realistically worked out. Others are little more than shopping lists or statements of intent. Sometimes a disregard ot the economic consequences may make such plans prohibitively expensive, or indeed prevent them from succeeding at all. But they cannot be measured by economic yardsticks alone. Just as the whole system of modifications of strict economic interest known as aid is taken—and offered—for political reasons, so in the internal sphere the uneconomic element in programmes of development and diversification are justified by politics too.

The inevitability, and the legitimacy also, of this approach is worth insisting on. Much of the state control introduced by new African governments is assumed by some Westerners and also by Communists to be more "Marxist", more "anti-Western" even, than in fact it is. This gives rise to misunderstandings. Perhaps more serious is the tendency of many donors to condemn most African industrial aspirations, and even some of the agricultural diversification, as "uneconomic". Observers in developed countries, and especially in former metropolitan powers, cannot all be expected to sympathize with political aims like economic independence and national prestige. But if these are recognized as legitimate goals of policy, the direction of economic effort towards such goals comes to seem comprehensible, if not always wise.

The methods of attaining greater economic independence and prosperity chosen by African leaders diverge externally above all on the extent to which they are willing to rely on the former colonial power, and internally on the degree of "socialism" and governmental control they are willing to introduce. These divergences mainly reflect the differing political views of the various leaders. But they also partly stem from differing estimates of the economic consequences.

This difference was dramatized, in the period after Ghana's independence and before that of the Ivory Coast, by what was known as Houphouet's bet with Nkrumah. The Ghanaian leader believed that a state-managed economy at home, and a militantly independent foreign policy and acceptance of Soviet and other aid abroad, were the best way to economic sovereignty and prosperity. The Ivory Coast leader, with much the same absolute one-party political system, put his money on free economy, the encouragement of capitalist enterprise and reliance on French aid, even at the price of less independence. He bet his neighbour, in effect, that over the next ten years the Ivory Coast would make greater progress than Ghana as a result. Here Monsieur Houphouet Boigny, apart from his political preferences, was gambling on French aid and investment continuing at the same high rate, and on Ghana doing less well because of her intransigent attitude towards Western governments and private capital. In the event the context has already changed. The Ivory Coast has become politically independent; and there are signs that the new state will by one means or another play a larger part in directing its economy than seemed likely five years ago. The Ghanaian Government has shown its willingness to collaborate with Western governments and private enterprise over the large-scale Volta project, and at the same time to obtain aid both from the East and from the West. Perhaps as time goes on the different roads chosen by the two neighbours will tend to converge.

Chapter Six

EDUCATION AND THE ELITE

IT is generally recognized, by Africans and by the experts brought in to advise them, that the prime requirement to move forward into the modern world is more education. Every newly independent African government intends and plans to provide more schooling and technical training at every level: some governments naturally with a greater sense of urgency than others. Almost every prominent African, and especially those who do not hold hereditary positions, owes his personal rise to his education; and a much higher proportion of educated Africans hold positions of authority than is the case in more developed societies. They consequently see education as the ladder up out of the morass of backwardness, poverty and sickness of African society, not only for individuals but for the community as a whole. The advantages of education, and the advancement it brings, are no less clear to the uneducated. Visitors to contemporary Africa are impressed by the eagerness of many Africans to learn, and by their often pathetic but none the less encouraging efforts to teach themselves.

Some observers, both African and foreign, have seen in this hunger for education, this belief in the importance of learning the ways of the white man's modern world, a reflection of the great stress which almost all African societies lay on transmitting to the next generation the accumulated experience and traditions of the community. Young men and women were—and are—taught how to master a hostile environment, and how to behave in adult society, often in conditions of personal endurance and hardship. What Africans are now looking for, these observers feel, is a similar initiation into the know-how and the values of the modern world; and it is in this light that they value education. To the extent that this is true —and it seems to me to represent one aspect of the African approach to education—it is a pity that Western education has not been able to make more use of traditional African systems of instruction, but has felt obliged to set them aside and even to combat them. Africans eager for a Western education have been quite as insistent on the breach as Western missionaries and educational experts.

As a result of this general and fervent interest, a great deal has been written about education in Africa. The subject has been carefully studied by commissions and by individual experts. The purpose of this chapter is not to summarize these writings, but rather to point to those aspects of the question that are particularly relevant to an understanding of the present context in tropical Africa.

During the period of colonial rule the education and technical training of Africans—the whole business of equipping them to run a modern society, as opposed to the simpler societies that existed before colonialism— necessarily devolved largely on the colonial governments, missionaries and commercial enterprises which for one reason or another felt impelled to undertake the task. It is scarcely surprising that this education reflects the needs and prejudices of these white institutions.

Missionary education was and is largely altruistic and humanitarian. Essentially religious, with literary and medical and social overtones, it is principally concerned with weaning Africans—individuals or whole communities—away from their tribal ways of life, or if this has already happened with giving them something more spiritually satisfying to take its place. In this basic respect the work of the Christian missionaries is strictly comparable to that of the traders and others who spread Islam, and with it hygiene, literacy and new loyalties. Many missionaries see this. But the Christian missions inevitably also spread a familiarity with the white man's technological world: his languages, his standards and his skills. This Islam has not offered in our time, though it certainly did so in the past and may come to do so again.

The training given by commercial enterprises is in most cases designed to increase the usefulness of the employee to the enterprise concerned. But since by their nature the mechanical, clerical and administrative skills concerned were precisely those needed in advanced societies but lacking in Africa, the process has been highly beneficial. Its benefits can most clearly be seen in those areas where the incentive to train Africans has not been lessened by the availability of non-African employees, who either have or can more easily acquire the needed skills, and where there has been no political or other objection to giving such training to Africans. Whatever economic and social organization the various new African states adopt for themselves after independence, they will clearly need all and much more than the skills which a small proportion of their citizens have acquired through training by foreign commercial enterprises.

The colonial governments had by about 1900 established their authority in tropical Africa. In the early stages they were in no position to accept the responsibility for education. But however much such administrations relied on missionaries to provide education in its more restricted sense, and on private enterprise to impart such technical and agricultural skills as it found expedient, all of them recognized that education lay within their purview. More recently the rapid growth of African demand for education, the increased sense of responsibility among colonial governments, the prospect of approaching self-government and Africanization and the lack of means on the part of missionary and other private enterprise have all forced governments to step in as the main agents and purveyors of education.

Colonial governments would all have liked to provide increased educational facilities; and their African successors are even more eager to do so. The limiting factor is and has been money. Locally raised revenue is preempted by other needs which seem to governments, colonial and independent, more urgent even than more education. A large proportion of both the money and the trained personnel must in most cases be obtained from outside. (This is of course the great attraction of missionary education for governments in Africa: they supply teachers and funds.) And so, with outside help, the independent governments of Africa have in almost every case stepped up the latterly much expanded programmes of the colonial administrations from which they took over. They are committed to more expansion still; in some cases to universal primary and secondary education.

The problems which confront the new governments in expanding their educational systems vary to some extent according to the different legacies they have inherited from the three colonial powers. It is worth looking at these in turn.

In the British territories the Colonial Office in London and the Colonial Governments on the spot made considerable efforts in the latter period of their authority to produce enlightened educational policies. The decentralized British system, the widely differing stages of cultural advance of various African people, and the presence or absence of European and Asian settlers all led to a diversified pattern; but a degree of co-ordination was achieved. The Advisory Committee on Native Education in Tropical Africa was set up in London in 1925. After the Second World War more money was made available for education in Africa, co-ordinated by the Inter-University Council and other advisory committees. The general principle was to establish primary education as a solid base on which to build. This purpose was almost everywhere achieved. As a result, the governments of former British territories find themselves with an extensive primary school system. According to the UNESCO working paper prepared for the Conference of African States on the Development of Education in 1961 this compared adequately in most cases with similar primary systems in Latin America and South-East Asia. But secondary education is much less developed. This is the bottleneck. University and college opportunities, in and outside Africa, are broadly adequate for the few children who get through secondary school and are willing and able to continue their studies. Since European education began later in East than in West Africa, even less secondary education is available there.

The three ex-Belgian countries, the Congo, Rwanda

and Burundi, have been left with an even more extensively developed primary network, which gives some schooling to three-quarters of the children of primary school age. But the Belgian secondary programme was even less expanded than the British; and consequently there is a very small educated élite.

The core of the problem in both the ex-British and ex-Belgian countries is how to expand the secondary system. For various reasons so few Africans stay through it to the level of University entrance, that enough or perhaps more than enough University places are likely to remain available, in Africa or elsewhere, for all who qualify. The rapid Africanization of government service and other walks of life creates such a demand for college graduates that few are available for teaching. But secondary schools need teachers who have graduated with a degree at least from a training college: otherwise standards fall. The governments of ex-British territories have decided that they must accept some fall in standards in the short run, as the price of expansion. As a result of rapid growth, in Ghana today only a third of secondary school teachers have these minimum qualifications, in Nigeria perhaps not more than a quarter. Standards will have to drop in the same way for a time in East Africa and in the Belgian territories.

The French, on the contrary, concentrated on producing a highly educated and assimilated élite in considerable numbers by African standards; and it is to this élite that they have now turned over power. While achieving this, the French made less effort to disseminate primary education widely. At the time of Ghana's independence in 1957 the proportion of children in primary schools in British

West Africa was about five times that in the French West African Federation. By now perhaps a quarter of the primary age-group in the eight French successor states are enrolled.

The former French colonies provide the most striking instance in independent tropical Africa of new states recognizing the advantage of accepting money and personnel for education on a very large scale from outside; sometimes even to the point of leaving the former colonial power in substantial control of their educational system. The offer which these new governments have accepted, the massive support in funds and teachers which the French state educational system still assigns to schools in its former colonies, is on a far more comprehensive and generous scale than outside aid to education in the other new African states. This is not a new system, but a continuation of an existing one. When these countries were part of Overseas France, it seemed natural to French Governments to spread the net of the French state educational machine over the almost wholly uneducated territories of Greater France: although much more thinly and selectively than in the more advanced European metropolis. This use of the French system seemed especially suitable because the aim was assimilation, and the language and civilization to be taught were those of France herself. The metropolitan curriculum could be used virtually without change. The teaching and administrative staff, who depended on the centralized French Ministry of Education, were assigned anywhere within the network (unlike those in British and American government schools, who are locally recruited and cannot simply be posted to schools overseas). The continuation of these arrangements has made it possible for the ex-French tropical African governments (including Madagascar) to employ some 7,000 French experts in their primary and secondary educational systems. The new countries obtain in this way large numbers of competent teachers which they would scarcely be able to recruit on the open market; and the French Government at present asks them to repay only about a fifth of the cost to the French tax-payer of the teacher's maintenance. The African governments regard the import of teachers on this scale as a temporary expedient; and when negotiating with the French Government about educational aid they all lay great stress on plans for training African teachers.

The problem of how to expand the secondary school system fast enough, which plagues the heirs of the British and Belgian systems, is at present less acute for the former French countries. For one thing fewer children come up from the fewer primary schools. And for another large numbers of highly trained French teachers are available for the secondary schools, and will no doubt continue to be furnished until competent Africans can take their places. The key question in these countries, around which controversy is likely to turn increasingly, is how far an education so French in its conception and its detail adequately serves African needs. The evidence seems to me to be that the better French educators appreciate the legitimacy of this question as clearly as do all but the most impatient Africans; and are searching for ways of adapting their educational system and curriculum to meet both the very different requirements of the new African nations and the wishes of the Africans concerned.

It will take time to see the results of the decisions about

education which must now be made. For the new governments of tropical Africa must not only overcome educational bottlenecks and deficiencies with such outside help
as they can obtain. They must also decide what sort of
education their countries require. Modern educational
experts who look at the educational systems inherited
from the colonial period, both governmental and private,
make two major criticisms of them. They are too bookish,
and too little concerned with Africa, to meet adequately
the needs of the new nations.

There is no doubt that in the past both missionary and
government-furnished education has been literary, spiritual and clerical. It was designed to train priests and
ministers; teachers, clerks and civil servants; and at a
higher level lawyers, doctors, politicians. It dispensed the
cultural and spiritual values of the colonizing power. But
it rarely passed on to Africans the technical knowledge
that gave the West its material superiority, or even the
ancillary crafts. And it certainly did not teach Africans the
history, geography and civilization of their own countries. Only in British territories were vernacular languages
used to any significant extent in schools. Africans were
brought up as provincial members of a distant culture, and
largely on its spiritual and bookish aspects. Sir Eric Ashby,
who headed the Commission on Post-Secondary and
Higher Education in Nigeria, has described the image of
education in West Africa in these terms. "The first schools
were not among unsophisticated tribes, but among
emancipated slaves. Therefore, pioneer teachers were not
faced with problems of cultural reconciliation between a
stable traditional society and the new Christian communities they were there to create. And as for associating

the saw, plane, and spade with the Bible, the very last thing emancipated slaves wanted to learn at school was practical skills or agriculture: they wanted the bookish education which could release them from manual labour. Therefore, both teacher and pupil conspired to identify education with books, literature and the exotic symbols of European culture. Furthermore, since the only door to advancement was through the mission school, even up to the present day most of the intellectuals of West Africa are men who inevitably have been torn up from their social roots, indoctrinated with a new religion and an unfamiliar code of ethics and encouraged from childhood to disregard their past."

Until recently Western-educated Africans have been among the loudest to insist that this should continue to be so. They did not want to be fobbed off with an inferior, more "practical" education than Europeans, or held within the little prison of their own local language and civilization, cut off from the more advanced world outside. "We want higher education to be exactly equal to that of the metropolis: we want a metropolitan curriculum", declared a Guinean Deputy in Paris shortly after the last war. And in Ghana, when the independent government established English as the general medium of instruction in primary schools, it asserted that the British policy of using a number of vernaculars in the first years of school had been inspired by the imperialist aim of dividing Ghanaians so as to make them easier to rule.

This resolve to master what the white man teaches his own children is widespread among Africans. Many of them do it very well. Of the hundreds of students in British Africa who try for a London University degree, for instance, about four in every five pass, which is much higher than the proportion for external candidates in the U.K. Naturally many Africans want to give their children similar opportunities, either in the former "metropolis" or elsewhere. The moral and teleological issues involved —the justification of individuals evolving beyond their community into citizens of the world, and indeed the legitimacy of emigration from one society to another—are beyond the scope of this book.[1] But certainly so far as the new African governments are concerned the aim of acquiring the white man's learning is understandable and justified so long as it is concerned with those aspects of advanced civilization which are relevant to producing modern African nations. And high among the technical accomplishments necessary for the understanding of the modern world is familiarity with a major international language.

There is no doubt that the pattern of African education today, and especially higher education, is not solely directed towards imparting the scientific and technological skills which a modern community requires, along with enough of the accumulated political and spiritual experience of other cultures to make up for the deficiencies of an inadequate African past. Its Western flavour goes considerably beyond what this aim would require. It is not fully explained even by the influence of inertia and continuity on the educational curriculum, the effect of Western subsidies and teachers, and the desire of the new governments to send a proportion of their abler new

[1] Even so, I do not wish to conceal my personal belief in the advantages to mankind of emigration, especially of the highly educated.

students profitably to universities in advanced countries with high and specialized admission standards. We must also note the opposition by many individual Africans to an "Africanization" of the subject-matter of education corresponding to the desired Africanization of the teaching staff and of the new nations generally.

Not only this. African governments have shown resistance and even resentment at suggestions by educational advisers from outside that a greater effort should be made to train the medium skills that the new nations so desperately require in fields like medicine and agronomy, instead of producing a few very eminent experts. The basic premise of these advisers, that education should be an integral part of a society and responsive to its needs, is acceptable to educated African opinion and indeed fits in very well with current views about nation-building. But the specific recommendations are often rejected as unpalatable: for two reasons. The overt and very real reason is that the targets recommended fall below the best achieved in more advanced countries, and so seem to relegate Africans to an inferior status. The less often cited reason is that many Africans see education as a means for individuals to escape up and out of the backwardness that besets the continent, into the international company of highly civilized men. They do not want to devote their lives to agricultural instruction, or preventive medicine; they want positions of respect, comfort and authority, if possible in the capital city with its amenities and the company of their fellows. There is great relevance in the observation quoted by Mr George Kimble in his *Tropical Africa*: "There is often some contempt for the illiterate peasant and no marked enthusiasm for rural occupations which would throw the educated man among such people. . . . There is little acknowledgment that the illiterate to whom education has been denied may include amongst their number many who are endowed with an intellectual potential at least equal to that of many university students. There is no widespread pity or sympathy for the illiterate."

The interest of the new and emerging societies clearly is to achieve both these ends. The governments must, here as in so many other fields, strike a reasonable balance with the limited means, domestic and foreign, at their disposal. They will want to produce distinguished scholars, in the arts as in the sciences. But the demands of education and medicine, of administration and industry, and above all the need to improve and diversify the agriculture by which most Africans live and which forms the bulk of most African countries' exports, must also somehow be met.

Moreover, opinions about Western influence in education are slowly evolving too. The new generation of Africans must surely, many Africans now argue, be trained not as scholars or experts merely, but as citizens. They must not be hangers-on of either the culture or the technology of the more advanced countries, but Africans. Cannot Africans draw on Western educational experience and on foreign aid for all that they need to equip the next generation as competent citizens of the modern world, and then use it for African purposes? An increasing number of Western-educated Africans are beginning to ask themselves whether, even if alien curricula continue to be faithfully copied, the values inculcated ought somehow to be African ones: both because Africa's new consciousness of herself demands this and because these values, if they are to be acceptable and effective, must link modern and educated Africans both with their own past and also with the rest of their own society. By "African values" educated Africans rarely mean, I believe, either some mystical emanation of the "African personality" or a refurbishing of primitive beliefs and tribal lore. It is rather a question of expressing the generally accepted values of civilization in an idiom and with an emphasis more acceptable to Africans than the formulations we have evolved for ourselves in the West or others elsewhere.

An educational system must be judged not only by its aims and its content, but also by its results. The search for new educational policies and objectives which correspond more closely to the basic aims of the new African governments raises in a direct form the question: What is the nature of the élite so far produced by the colonial system of education in Africa?

The origins of this élite in colonial times have been indicated in Chapter Two. Today it is made up essentially of those Africans who for one reason or another took kindly to Westernization (though not of course to pro-Western political sympathies) and who made the most of their opportunities, especially in school. In this way they have fitted themselves to manage and direct the affairs of a modern state. The positions they have obtained are the rewards above all of adaptability and perseverance—for both these qualities are required to assimilate a new, more advanced and very different civilization. And it is these qualities in themselves, as well as the technical qualifications they have helped their possessors to acquire, which have enabled the élite to graduate into the influential and lucrative positions which they now hold.

This book has been largely concerned with the desire of the élite, who now find power in their hands, to build modern, independent African nations: to free themselves and their countrymen from European domination by mastering the indispensable techniques of the advanced world and adapting them to Africa's different requirements. This is, in general, the aim professed by educated Africans; and these are no doubt the goals that most of them sincerely see themselves as striving for. But the misgiving is frequently expressed, and not least by thoughtful Africans themselves, that alongside these fine general aspirations to see Africans take the place of Europeans and manage affairs in the interests of the new nation rather than those of the colonizers, there is the much more direct and personal desire to step into the white man's shoes and run things in their own interests. We have seen that, as is natural, the African élite want the way of life displayed to them by their European rulers. As these Europeans were usually men of some ability, who were compensated for their expatriation by a higher standard of living than they would normally have enjoyed at home, the way of life displayed to Africans had been an impressive one. To what extent, the critics ask, is the real goal of the African élite to enjoy for themselves the white man's authority, his say-so, his house, his car, his servants, even his "home leave" in Europe? How far do their wives who care less about nation-building, want to step into the shoes of the white women, both for the prestige and the ease of it? More seriously and ominously, how far has control of the new nations' destinies passed into the hands of a small, Westernized ruling class, divorced by a wide gulf in its everyday life and its outlook from the mass of the people it governs and determined to keep to itself the power it has obtained and to perpetuate its oligarchic rule?

These are legitimate questions; but they must not be allowed to imply their own answers. No doubt it was among the dearest ambitions of many educated Africans to live like the Europeans in their midst. And there can be little doubt also of the conservatism and *arrivisme* of many of the leading groups in contemporary Africa, once they have come to power. Many of the radical younger generation, full of revolutionary impatience before they attain office, quickly adopt the attitude of their elders once they find themselves on the way up the ladder. The conspicuous affluence by African standards of many Africans in office, and the "expatriate" and occasionally semi-regal levels of personal living enjoyed by the less austere rulers are evidence of the same spirit as the insistence by the new governments on authority, order and stability. There may be accidents, Putsches, overturned governments: as the recent history of several African states reminds us. But the new regimes that have come to power intend and expect to stay there.

It is not a question of whether the present leaders of these governments incline towards radicalism and socialism, or prefer private enterprise and continued close association with the former colonial power. Almost without exception the new regimes mobilize the whole élite to build the new nation, except those individuals who have been politically proscribed. There is no provision for a democratic alternative: virtually all are in the mood of *j'y suis, j'y reste*. Many of the new governments in practice regard with some indulgence the perquisites and pickings that may go with office, or come the way of the mobilized élite. And among the perquisites of office, certainly, indeed among the perquisites of Westernization in general, they include the comfort and affluence which the Western rulers of tropical Africa enjoyed in colonial times. This attitude is reinforced by the sentiment in traditional African societies that the prestige and authority of a ruler were marked not only by the power he wielded but also by the state he kept.

The desire to remain in office, to retain power for the élite and for the party, is not confined to those African societies where personal standards of luxury are high at the top. In the more puritan and "socialist" states, where both personal and official consumption is severely and effectively limited, the ruling group is equally anxious to perpetuate itself in power, equally *arriviste* in other aspects of behaviour. And the angry young men who denounce "undemocratic" standards of wealth and consumption normally advocate a still more authoritarian regime.

Let us recognize, then, that the rulers of the new African states, and their followers, mean to stay on top; and that some of them, and especially their wives, mean to have a good time. Does this indicate that we are witnessing the formation of a new ruling class, comparable to those of the Middle East and Latin America? The answer, so far as it is not too early to make even a provisional guess, is: probably not. A number of reasons militate against the formation of such a class structure in modern African society.

The first reason is that the élite have not so far been chosen from a small group. They come from a wide range of backgrounds. Those who have struggled up to something like the top of a new nation are connected with almost every ethnic and social group in it, and have got there by dint of personal skill and application. In Africa the ties of the "extended family" are much greater than in the more disintegrated and individualistic societies of the West. The great majority of the élite, in government and out, are in close contact with their relatives and indeed their clansmen, and pass on to them considerable sums of money and other facilities. The personal barriers necessary to the formation of a distinct caste are scarcely there.

Secondly, the basis of power of the Middle Eastern and South American aristocracies has been the large scale and hereditary ownership of land. Though some of the African élite have high standards of consumption, they normally do not have this territorial basis, and usually show little signs of obtaining it. So far, it is the perquisites of political office that Africans have acquired. The conditions of African society, especially the prevailing forms of land ownership, which are usually communal or something akin in practice to peasant proprietorship, often with matriarchal overtones, make the amassing of large landed estates unlikely. Nor, as we saw when discussing the prospects of capitalism, are considerable fortunes of other kinds forming on a significant scale. Industrial and commercial activity too seems to be tending rather in the direction of state control or even ownership than of private industrial empires.

Nor do we find in the new societies of tropical Africa a powerful and entrenched Church or army which in other countries often uphold the position of the ruling oligarchy.[1] Indeed the army, whether in the control of a traditional ruling class or a group of young and revolutionary "élite" officers, dominates so many countries in other underdeveloped areas of the world today, and is a significant factor in so many others, that it is remarkable that in tropical Africa this is not the rule. Armies in the new African countries are usually small organizations, often trained by foreigners and in most cases willing to obey the new governments, in spite of sporadic and sometimes prolonged mutinies. What will develop in the future, it is too early to say.

A third factor militating against the formation of an élite oligarchy is the rapid extension of education in Africa. The conditions that produced this small educated —often highly educated—élite stratum, distinguished from the mass of its fellow-citizens by its "modernization", are disappearing as a new generation grows up in which "modernization" and education are more widely spread. The educational efforts now being made by almost every African government will lessen this difference still further. No doubt the children of the present élite will receive a better education than the average; and because they come from more literate and educated homes they will, as a rule, take more advantage of it than their fellows from less advanced homes. And when their education is finished, no doubt nepotism as well as their better educational qualifications will secure them a large proportion of influential jobs. But this is a widespread phenomenon; and hardly amounts to the

[1] An exception is the Sudan, where religious and military leaders have dominated the new republic since independence : for this purpose the Sudan must be reckoned a part of the Middle East.

formation of a distinct class in the sense we have been discussing.

On balance, therefore, it does not seem likely that a small governing caste, cut off from the rest of the population, will develop out of the present educated élite. The danger is more likely to lie in the perpetuation of a party oligarchy: willing enough to take in new recruits of ability, but assuring to itself a monopoly of effective power and a generous share of material privilege. This is always a danger with party structures of the kind now so familiar in Africa, whatever their political complexion and aims. It is well described in Mr Milovan Djilas' *Novii Klass*. But this danger too, though inherent in the political system, is far from inevitable. The spread of education will not only tend to ensure that the party is recruited from a wider range of candidates, but will also diminish the difference between those who are chosen and those who are not. All any outsider can say is that as Africans struggle with this worldwide phenomenon, they are likely to give it a decided twist of their own.

In turn, the nature and effects of education in Africa today are mainly due to the selective training of a few Africans in the very different and more advanced techniques and values of the West. Those selected in this way have been individually emancipated and detribalized, and many of them have been educated well above the average level in the West itself. But the numbers of Africans so trained are still far too few to man the multifarious skilled positions in a modern state. And the material and psychological gulf between them and most of their fellow-countrymen is dangerously wide, though their links with

African society remain closer than a casual observer might suppose.

The diffusion of modern education, especially at the secondary level, among much wider circles of Africans will help to remedy many of the ills we have been examining. As independence is consolidated, the leaders of the new states will no doubt come increasingly to see the need for an educational system more specifically adapted to the needs and the outlook of modern Africa. They may listen to those experts[1] who urge them to develop something which is less a lavish and often irrelevant copy of a Western model: something less bookish, more technical, and more concerned with African society. It is more education that must help the new governments to deal with the technological gap and achieve the increased production necessary for economic independence, as well as to combat malnutrition and disease. And especially it should help to solve the problem of the élite divorced by its education from the rest of the population; which is in essence the problem of the reintegration of African society. It is not surprising that almost all the new governments lay great stress on a rapid increase of education.

The African countries cannot yet produce for themselves the facilities they need for an effective expansion of their educational systems. They recognize that for some years at least they must obtain help from abroad over matters like trained teachers, buildings, expert advice, and scholarships for further training of Africans in advanced countries. These facilities foreign governments are very ready to supply, for the reasons listed in Chapter Five, though not always in large enough volume to satisfy

[1] Sir Eric Ashby is a good example

African needs. But education is not merely the provision of facilities. Unless it also imparts a sense of values, it degenerates into mere vocational training. And in the Africa of tomorrow these values are likely to be more specifically African. But neither the search for African values nor the maintenance of very high technical standards are likely to stand in the way of the diffusion of education in Africa. Here the instinct of the African leaders seems justified; this is a case where *le mieux est l'ennemi du bien*.

Chapter Seven

THE GENESIS OF FOREIGN POLICY

THE need for trade-and-aid is so enormously important to the new African countries, and the political issues it raises are so vital to the process of nation-building, that much of the foreign policy of the new governments is inevitably taken up with these questions. But there are other issues in the field of external affairs which also occupy much of the new governments' attention. Such issues are Pan-Africanism; neutralism; the desire to liberate the rest of the continent from alien rule; and the desire to establish their position in the eyes of the world. It is to these issues that we must now turn.

In one sense the basic aim of anti-colonialism is to re-establish the "foreignness" of Africa in the face of the colonizing power; and the business of an anti-colonial movement was to propagate this sentiment. The reopening of those other direct contacts which the colonial occupation had in effect closed, was one of the purposes which independence would make possible. The first beginnings of foreign policy are therefore to be found in the dissociation of the African "freedom movements", and indeed of political groupings and parties that were not at first consciously secessionist, from the imperial system in which they found themselves. Some African leaders of course, especially in areas of indirect rule like the Emirates of Northern Nigeria, never lost their sense of foreignness towards the colonial power. But in most territories there was a period when colonial rule was acknowledged; and the sense of foreignness was more firmly if inarticulately alive among the mass of tribal villagers than among those who came more into contact with the colonizers.

This sense of distinctness from the colonizing power was fostered by the British system of encouraging each territory to regard itself as a separate entity, destined to achieve "self-government within the Commonwealth" some day in the future. White settlers might think of themselves as "British overseas"; but the Africans did not. British African leaders were not elected to the Parliament at Westminster, and very rarely appointed to posts in Britain. Loyalties were not diverted from the embryo state to Britain itself. To think about the attainment of this status, following the example of India; to propose and discuss policies for the period after independence; all this was regarded by the colonial authorities as respectable, if sometimes a little premature. As the moment of independence drew nearer, embryo foreign offices were set up, and young men posted to British embassies abroad to learn the professional techniques which independent diplomacy would require. The arguments between the African freedom movements and the colonial authorities were over timing, and over constitutional issues (especially in territories with non-African minorities). Since ultimate self-government was not in question, the feeling of the British African leaders, that the time left before independence was much shorter than the authorities believed, or that at least it could and should be made so, was rather one of degree than kind.

The political leaders of the French territories on the other hand belonged to the small apparently assimilated élite, who in spite of certain occasional misgivings usually seemed to think of themselves as French and sat in the French Parliament or even in French governments. Here we may trace the beginnings of dissociation in the meetings of African deputies attached to different French parties in Paris from 1946 onwards, which led among other results to the formation of the R.D.A. Dissociation was carried a stage further once the idea became explicit that it did not much matter what parties made up the governmental coalition in France so long as they passed the legislation desired by Africans. These activities were usually regarded as no more than an example of the familiar inter-party lobby; just as the intellectual search for what constituted the distinctive essence of the African spirit, the quest for Négritude, seemed no more than the self-expression of a large but hitherto not very vocal cultural minority within the French system. The French African leaders themselves certainly did not proclaim their activities as moves towards political independence. But this was in fact the direction in which they were being impelled.

The next stage, as monolithic parties and their leaders gradually established their dominance over the different territories which made up the British and French Colonial Empires in tropical Africa, was the establishment of relations between these parties and particularly between their leaders. Within the French West African Federation, for instance, even those parties which aimed at a federal political machine developed in fact on territorial lines. From an early stage there was conflict between those groups in favour of the Federation and those who opposed it. Different territories wished to maintain the Federation for different reasons. They included the Senegalese who benefited from having the federal capital of Dakar in their territory; and the poorer territories like the Soudan, Upper Volta and Dahomey who depended on federal subsidies and on employment outside their own borders. Opposed to Federation were the richer territories. Especially the Ivory Coast resented the federal system as remote from its interests, as a barrier between itself and France, and a drain on its slightly greater but still inadequate resources for the benefit of territories even more impoverished than itself. As a result of this and other differences, the party leaders found themselves manoeuvring with and against each other, and with or against the government in Paris, like autonomous states within a general system. These coalitions, reversals of alliances, and occasional interferences in each other's "domestic affairs" took a stage further the evolution of embryo foreign policies.

This process is worth examining in slightly greater detail, because French West Africa provides an exceptionally clear example of it. By 1956 the R.D.A. was being subjected to particular strain. Both the Suez affair, which Monsieur Houphouet Boigny of the Ivory Coast, the party's leader-in-chief, and Monsieur Modibo Keita of the Soudan defended as Ministers in the French Government in Paris, and the French Government's Algerian policy were causes of dissension enough. But the main issue was the basic aim of the French Government, made manifest first in the *loi-cadre* of 1956 and then in the *Communauté* of 1958, to disband the Federation by stages and to substitute a system of eight autonomous provinces each radially linked to France. The champion of this policy was Houphouet Boigny. But his two principal followers broke with him on this issue. Sékou Touré of Guinea, who commanded the most effective and radical territorial party in the R.D.A., led his country out of the *Communauté* altogether in the referendum of 1958, because the new French constitution provided specifically that no member of the *Communauté* could be independent. And Modibo Keita, the leader of the similar territorial party of the R.D.A. in the Soudan, joined with the Senegalese leaders in opposition to Houphouet Boigny to form the Mali Federation within the *Communauté*. After Houphouet Boigny, with some French support, had detached the other three prospective members of the Mali Federation (Upper Volta, Niger and Dahomey) by offers of greater inducements, Keita and the Senegalese demanded and obtained from France the right to independence. But within a few months of acceding to international sovereignty in 1960 the Federation split into its two component parts; and Keita and Houphouet Boigny (now also independent) began to feel their way cautiously back towards each other.

British West Africa was different enough from French to mask the underlying similarity of the relations between the parties and their leaders. The four territories were geographically separate, and proceeded towards political independence at different paces, as well as having virtually no formal links. It therefore seemed much more natural and indeed inevitable that each of them should go its own way, and that such common services as the West African Currency Board and the West African air line should be dissolved into national components by mutual consent. But we may see in the rivalry that troubles the relations between the leaders and parties of Ghana and Nigeria, which dates from the period before full independence, a feeling similar to those differences which divided the French territories from one another and gradually made them increasingly aware of their invidual identities. Nigeria has remained united in a Federation, and a very large one. Within this framework it is instructive to note the pattern of alliances and disagreements between the dominant parties and their leaders in the constituent states. This is the sort of pattern that might have evolved had French West Africa too remained a federation.

The British East African scene seems too unclear to see yet what federal or other relationship may emerge or even what may be the constituent territories of the area. But the network of party relationships between the different parties and their leaders is already beginning to shift as interests and aspirations change in the course of establishing independence. In the Belgian Congo the parties scarcely had time to form before they were all engulfed in the unexpected tidal wave of independence; but even so the separation of Katanga and other provinces from the Centre and from each other was expressed by embryo parties and their leaders according to what may be called the classic African pattern. It offers a close parallel to developments in French West Africa which is clear to the African leaders concerned.

These relations between parties in different territories of the same imperial system, and the negotiations with the colonial power, served to strengthen the sense of separate identity in the emerging states, and to give them some experience of what might be called external affairs. But they were essentially "in the family". Foreign policy proper only begins when the parties and their leaders have

contacts with external powers. Here the French territories offer little valuable evidence. The contacts with
Communism did not normally go beyond the French
Communist Party and an occasional visit behind the Iron
Curtain. Some French African leaders were in correspondence with the Ghanaian leaders—President Senghor, for
instance, has a long-standing acquaintance with President
Nkrumah—but the French leaders were not at that time
thinking in terms of their own political independence.
The leaders in the Trust Territories had some experience
of the UN. The most conspicuous example was President
Olympio of Togo. He was in independent contact with
the Ghanaian leaders in the early '50s, and established an
independent position for himself at the UN by means of
which he was able to procure UN supervision of the Togo-
lese elections and even of the compilation of the electoral
rolls: which brought him and his party to power.

Political leaders in the British territories had at an early
stage an extensive system of contacts outside the immediate British fold. They were in touch not only with
countries like India, which for this purpose was counted
as outside official bounds; but also and most conspicuously with the United States. Some of these leaders have
been partly educated in the United States, like President
Nkrumah, or have American wives like Mr Karefa Smart
and Mr Mboya. But even where the ties are less strong,
many things attracted British African leaders to the U.S.
The possession of a common language, the precedent of
India, the American negroes, the anti-colonial sympathies
of most white Americans: all these attractions may be
summed up by saying that the United States were the
first colonies to liberate themselves from British political

control; and that a natural bond therefore unites the United States to other British colonies seeking their independence, more closely than to the colonies of other powers. To most Americans the aims of the British African leaders seemed legitimate and desirable. Even violence was felt to be justified as a last resort; although certainly the British, like the French, seemed ready enough to hand over power well before that. The British colonial authorities certainly had a keen sense of this special nexus. Their exasperation at the damage, which this forcing of the pace did to their own struggle to lay a solid foundation for future self-government, was also a factor in the approach of educated Africans to foreign relations. It doubtless had the beneficial effect of providing British Africans with an alternative range of contacts that were English-speaking but yet not identified with the colonial powers. But this was obtained at the price of hindering, until recently, effective collaboration between two powers who both wanted to achieve the same purpose of preparing African societies rapidly and responsibly for competent self-government.

The dangers that derive from moving too slowly towards independence are by now clear enough. So are the risks produced by what is superficially the opposite policy, but is in fact another consequence of overestimating the time in hand—the sudden realization that the moment for independence has come, and the resulting abrupt handing over of power and responsibility to those still unprepared for the task. Both types of difficulty underline the need for as long a weaning period as circumstances will allow. This is as true in foreign affairs as in other aspects of government. People do learn to swim, as when they are thrown in at the deep end; but they manage much better if they have been taught, or allowed to teach themselves, in time. The technical sides of foreign affairs can be taught by the "colonial tutor", and they need learning as much as any other technique. But the political ones cannot. Africans must learn these for themselves: though here again they can be helped by the metropolitan power in the stages immediately before and after political independence.

A carry-over from the period of anti-colonial struggle which continues to haunt the new African governments in their relations with the former colonial power and with other outside governments and organizations is the fear of "neo-colonialism". Some of these new countries are more able to stand on their own feet than others. The weaker governments are sometimes keenly aware of the need for budgetary support, sheltered markets, administrative stiffening and perhaps even military protection at least for several years to come. When this is forthcoming in adequate quantities and in manageable form only from the former colonizing power, and especially when it is available on the very generous scale offered by France, such governments may decide that discretion on the subject of their fears is the better part of sovereignty, and that if their independence is to be made into a reality they must take all the help they can get during the period of development. But even these weak and prudent governments are sensitive to the charge of neo-colonialism, which is overtly made by their neighbours, whispered by their own more radical countrymen, and present in their own breasts. What then is meant by neo-colonialism?

The expression itself was popularized by the Communist, particularly by the Soviet, propaganda machines. It has proved effective in Africa because it focuses certain fears, rather than objective realities. At the heart of these fears lies the suspicion that the colonial powers who have dispensed independence in Africa with fairly good grace and rather sooner than many people once expected, have conceded, or tried to concede, only the shadow of independence while retaining the substance of power in disguised forms. These imperial leopards, so the suspicion goes, cannot really have changed their spots. They cannot really have wanted self-government in Africa; indeed have not even acquiesced in it. Is it not their plan to yield over political forms, over internal government, over the flag and the glory, while retaining the essence of ultimate control by economic, strategic or other less obvious means? The belief that colonialism and all imperialism have economic exploitation as their principal motive, and that the maintenance of this exploitation is the only real interest of the imperialist powers, is a Marxist overtone, a rationalization of a more genuine and understandable African fear.

With the passage of time, and in the face of the evidence, the fear of neo-colonialism seems to be abating. It also finds itself in conflict with another African anxiety, that the outside world generally, and even the former colonial power, are less interested in tropical Africa than they were, or than Africans had supposed. May the aid, the privileged markets, even the "economic exploitation", in fact decline? May the new African countries be left to fend unduly much for themselves? None the less, neo-colonialism after formal independence is and will for some time remain an active bogey in many African minds; and interested parties will try to keep the fear alive. It is therefore much in the interest of the Western powers to demonstrate, more convincingly to African minds than they have so far done, that the imperial leopards really have lost most of their spots, and that the rest are fading.

Since the attainment of international sovereignty, the individual states of tropical Africa have had to come to grips with the practical problems of maintaining current external relations: to regulate their day-to-day inter-course with other sovereign states, and to work out ways and means of collaborating with those states that also wish to attain various specific objectives. In doing so they make a natural distinction in their minds between their relations with other tropical African countries, and especially with their neighbours and their fellow-members of the same former imperial system, who are so to speak in the same boat as themselves; and the different kind of relationship they have with the outside world.

All Africans feel in some degree the gravitational pull towards continental solidarity. They think of the new nations, or at any rate the negro ones, as all belonging to the same African family. It is not just a number of different states, it is Africa as a whole that is reasserting its independence. This general sense of solidarity, transcending national loyalties, is the basis of Pan-Africanism. The nagging awareness of many Africans that even the transfer of political sovereignty has not automatically made them wholly masters in their own houses is aggravated by the division of the area into a multiplicity of states, some medium sized but many of them very small in terms of population and resources. An important part of the strength of Pan-Americanism derives from the feeling that if the new African countries are to count for anything, if they are to make their influence felt and their wishes respected, if they are not to remain individual victims of neo-colonialism or of neglect, then they must act in concert.

This sense of the need to act together if anything of importance is to be achieved is naturally strongest where those emotional issues are involved that affect all Africans. The most obvious example is discrimination against Africans or people of African origin on account of their race, or anything that affects their dignity and standing in the world. Such discrimination is naturally felt to be a more immediate threat if it happens in Africa itself. Similarly peoples who have just emerged from colonial control, and leaders who have struggled, sometimes militantly, for independence, regard African solidarity to put an end to the remaining vestiges of colonialism in Africa as natural. In fact, the African states are easily mustered to diplomatic activity, in the United Nations and elsewhere, the effects of which should not be underestimated; but economic sanctions and other painful measures are naturally harder to organize. In an increasing number of other less emotional fields too the new African countries are finding it profitable to co-operate. Communications, currency, defence, even the stabilization of commodity prices and the marketing of certain products like coffee and groundnuts, have shown the advantages of concerted action.

In the general opinion of the present African leaders these purposes, including effective collaboration at the United Nations and in other international bodies, can best be organized within the framework of a league or union of African states. Under the general umbrella of this continent-wide union, states with particularly close affinities or reasons for collaboration can form smaller and more intimate groupings.

Such associations and unions are not what we should call federal structures. They do not involve any serious pooling of newly acquired sovereignty. Proposals to set up a federal state, with a single leader and an effective federal executive, which would reduce the new states to provinces of Pan-Africa, have been put forward by Ghana and others; but always decisively rejected. Nor has effective federalism been conspicuously more successful in the smaller groupings. The difficulties of the Mali Federation and the dissolution of the French Equatorial Union, and the sweetness of being the cock in their own backyard, have so far kept the French African leaders from setting up any formal confederation among themselves. Their *Union Africaine et Malgache* remains a loose association of French-speaking states which preserve their separate sovereignties, internationally and domestically. In East Africa we may see a federation of three or more ex-British states which under colonialism shared certain common services. But the wider grouping of "PAFMECSA" is not intended to be more than an association of states acting in concert. The Ghana-Guinea-Mali Union never got much beyond ideological solidarity, especially because the component states were geographically separated. The three countries were also members of the largely Arab "Casablanca Group"; which did no more than talk about constitutions and joint armed forces, while remaining in practice like the other groups a league or union of sovereign members. Some of these smaller unions may in time move towards becoming political communities, in the sense in which this term is now used in Europe. But most of their immediate aims can probably be attained without doing so.

Of more significance for Pan-African sentiments is the "Organization of African Unity" set up in Addis Ababa in May 1963. This league embraces or is expected to embrace all the states on the continent governed by Africans. It is a clear expression, arrived at after years of preliminary negotiation, of what African solidarity means in practice at this time, so far as formal organization is concerned. The terms of its Charter provide such a useful and authoritative statement of the policies and sentiments of the member governments, not merely on collaboration but on the aims it is expected to foster, that the text is printed as Appendix B to this book.

We may see from the nature and limits of the various negotiations for union in Africa that, while consciousness of African solidarity is a real force in some fields, it is out-weighed by local nationalism in others and especially the more intimate ones. The story of tropical Africa's attain-ment of independence shows clearly what a strong tend-ency there is for small areas to attain individual statehood, and how difficult it is to make close federations work successfully. There can be no mistaking the resolve of most African governments not to allow Pan-African sentiment to interfere with the process of building their individual nation on the pattern they have chosen—with the aid of Professor Wallerstein's "surgical clamps".

The counterpart of Pan-Africanism inside Africa is neutralism in relations with the outside, non-African world. Implicit in the whole anti-colonial movement is the desire to end the special relationship of an African territory with one particular overseas power. This inevitably involves not only complete internal self-government, but also the maintenance of direct relations at the discretion of the new state with other outside powers. It is in a sense the reversion, on the international plane, to the conditions which prevailed before the colonial partition and occupation of Africa in the 1880s. But there is one major difference. The new nations are themselves largely the creations of the colonial occupation and stand in a special and ambivalent relationship to the colonial power.

A first step in forming direct relations with the outside world is the establishment of working connexions, especially over matters like aid, with powers friendly to the colonial authorities. This process usually begins before the attainment of formal independence. It continues with the good offices and help of the former colonial power in the immediately following period. One conspicuous example of such arrangements is the introduction of U.S. aid and other activities into British territories, notably Nigeria, in the last stages of colonial responsibility. Another is the extensive arrangements which France has made with her partners in the European Economic Community, especially Federal Germany, to shoulder some of the economic burdens of providing aid, markets and other facilities to the former French dependencies by the device of associating them with the Community shortly before their independence.

This extension of the horizon is of course welcome to the emerging African countries. It goes some way to relieve the psychological claustrophobia which they inevitably felt in the period just before they attained international sovereignty. It also brings the welcome flavour of different advice and different ways of doing things to men sated by the restriction to one set of national contacts. The fumbling inexperience of some early efforts at collaboration with other countries, and the mutual irritation which is sometimes engendered, seem to African governments a small price to pay for the advantages of these new contacts.

A more difficult decision presents itself to the new African governments when they come to consider extending their relation still further, to countries which the former colonial power is not prepared to sponsor and which it and its friends may actively oppose. On the one hand the instinct for neutralism between the West and its political enemies, and the wish to become generally accepted members of international society, push the new states towards a wider circle of relationships. Governor Mennen Williams formulated the sentiment in a memorable phrase when he said that the new nations are not content to emerge into only half the world. Moreover, many of the countries in question, both among the neutrals and among the active opponents of the West, seem to have much to offer. In many cases they are apparently working for aims which appeal to the new African countries; and then some of them have advice, example, and even more concrete forms of aid to offer. On the other hand, as we saw in Chapter Five, each new government is keenly aware of the need to find where the overall net balance of advantage lies in its relations with the outside world. Each government must balance the political, psychological and more material advantages it may derive from these wider contacts against what it may lose, in trade-and-aid and in other forms of support and goodwill, from the former colonial power and the other nations of the West.

So we find that, with one or two conspicuous exceptions, the former British and French countries of tropical Africa have proceeded very cautiously in this matter of extending their contacts to the point of incurring the active displeasure of the major Western powers. Most of the British territories have been ready enough to establish diplomatic relations with Communist as well as neutralist countries: especially as they were not made aware of any British objection. But they have hesitated to sacrifice the goodwill of the West by entering into significant or disturbing commitments to Communist powers. They are inclined to prefer the devil they know, and his associates (who are turning out not to be so devilish after all, in this new post-colonial world), to the devils they don't know, but who seem to behave rather worse and to offer these new countries considerably less. Most of the former French countries have been even more careful: many of them still hesitate to establish even what might be called platonic relations with Communist countries. Where there have been exceptions to this general mood of caution there is usually a good reason. Guinea found herself at the critical start of her independent career denied aid by France and her friends on terms which her leaders considered acceptable; and felt obliged to come to terms with the Communist countries, with results which they have not found happy. In Ghana the President and many of his advisers feel especially strongly the need on general political grounds to maintain approximately equal relations with both sides in the struggle between the great power blocks. They did not until recently consider either the amount of aid Ghana received from the West, or the danger of losing it, large enough to make this political purpose seem dangerously unwise. Neither of these governments likes to think of itself today as more closely linked to the Communist powers than to the West.

If most of the African countries have hesitated to move too fast or too far in their relations with the enemies of the West, they have been more ready to identify them-selves with neutralists in other continents. Neutralism elsewhere corresponds to their own sentiment that newly independent states must avoid entangling alliances. The fulfilment of their national purpose means for them among other things that they should cease to be pawns or auxiliaries in a struggle which they feel is not really theirs. They want to dissociate themselves from the quarrels between the rival powers. In this respect one or two African leaders, including President Senghor of Senegal, have argued that the active ideological and material imperialisms of the United States and Russia are more redoubtable than the fading colonial or neo-colonial pur-poses of second-rank West European powers like France and Britain. Since changes in strategy and in outlook have also led the great powers to attach much less im-portance than previously to the value of the small African countries as auxiliaries, the new countries have not met the opposition they feared in associating with neutralist powers like India, Egypt or Yugoslavia.

This tendency to co-operate with other neutralists on certain specific international issues is by no means uni-versal among the new African governments. It may grow. But on the other hand the future of neutralism, of the kind formerly advocated by India, is less clear than it once appeared. Nobody in Africa now preaches the "Spirit of Bandoeng". It seems safe to say that the general desire of tropical Africans to dissociate themselves from the quarrels of the great powers extends to quarrels between the great powers of Asia too. There is no longer in any meaningful sense an "Afro-Asian bloc": certainly not with the implication that the African states accept the leadership of the Asian ones. On the contrary, though the governments of the new tropical African states may find it convenient to associate with certain Asian ones on issues like neutralism and anti-colonialism, most of them see little to envy or copy in Asia as a whole, though they may respect and be willing to learn from the achievements of individual countries in limited fields. Indeed "Asia" as a concept seems often to represent to educated Africans not so much an example as a vague threat; a continent which might somehow try to solve its overpopulation problems at the expense of Africa's still unused resources. Some outside observers have expressed concern that such fears might inhibit economic exchanges between African and Asian countries, or prevent people of Asian origin now in Africa, such as the Indians of East Africa or the "Syrians" of the West, from making their full contribution to the countries in which they live.

Both in their relations with other African states and with the rest of the world the governments of these new countries, and indeed their peoples too, are anxious to make good their claim to acceptance as full members of the community of nations on a basis of equality with everyone else. They want to be taken seriously. But most of them, and notably the ex-French states (none of which has a population much over four million and some of less than a million souls), are aware that they have now launched themselves into independence as small, poor and comparatively unknown members of international society. Their leaders realize that few people outside the circle of the former French Empire yet have a clear idea of what a country like Mali or the Central African Republic, for instance, is and represents. It therefore seems important to these governments to affirm their new nationhood internationally, to make people realize who and what these new countries are and what they stand for. This policy of *se faire valoir* seems necessary in order to increase their external effectiveness: to carry due weight in the councils of Africa and in the search for aid and other aims outside. It also strengthens a government's internal authority and prestige, and makes the citizens take their leaders more seriously. This is the value to new states of exchanges of state visits and ceremonial occasions. The politically conscious citizens of the new countries want to see their leaders photographed with those of other African countries and with the leaders of the great powers. This desire to make the new countries' presence felt in the world also partly explains the surprisingly large number of Embassies which they maintain in important capitals; and is one of the reasons behind the great efforts which African governments make to embellish their capital cities, so that they shall seem impressive and agreeable to visitors: in contrast with the disconcerting lack of amenities up country. The larger and more self-assured a country is, the less impelled its government feels to *se faire valoir* in this way. The Nigerian giant, sometimes accused by other Africans of a superiority-complex, is perhaps the best example.

In their search for ways to bring colonialism and discrimination to an end, in their desire to disentangle
themselves safely from the rivalries of the great powers
into an acceptable neutralism, and in their efforts to make
their existence an international reality, the most useful
instrument for the African governments is the United
Nations. Admission to the United Nations is for them the
ultimate and decisive form of international recognition.
Each Council and Assembly provides a forum, where
representatives of these countries can explain their policy
while the world listens. Their votes can be effective in
furthering causes like anti-colonialism where force would
be more risky and probably less effective. In the United
Nations all are equal; and was not the organization set up
to protect the weak against the strong? Into the bargain
the specialized agencies of the U.N., like the World Health
Organization and the Food and Agriculture Organization, and affiliated bodies like the World Bank, bring
substantial practical benefits to Africa, in a form eminently
acceptable to African national susceptibilities. And where
things go wrong, as they did in the Congo, the intervention of the United Nations can, in the opinion of many
and probably of most Africans, exercise a steadying effect
and prevent matters from being even worse. Moreover,
the African states make up between a quarter and a third
of the Organization's membership: a position greater than
their population or wealth or degree of technological
advance would have obtained for them in what one might
call an open international market. It is small wonder that
the United Nations commands such general support
among the new nations of Africa.

We can thus see that a connecting thread runs through

all the beads that make up the foreign policy of the new states. This thread is the desire to establish for Africa, as it emerges again into independence, a new and recognized position in the councils of the world which it did not have in the days before colonialism. The position they want is the one that seemed natural and desirable after independence to those Africans who worked under colonial rule to bring that rule to an end: the vision of a league of African states, neutral, respected and influential through their own solidarity. It is true that in the sober, workaday world of post-independence responsibilities and pressures the vision has been modified somewhat. Once in power the new governments have laid more stress on preserving individual state sovereignties, and in co-operating with the former colonial powers and their friends to solve the technical and economic problems that now loom so much larger than they did before the transfer of power. But in its essence it is still the same policy. Perhaps an obvious one for a group of countries with so much in common emerging into international statehood: but certainly one which has not been so successfully realized in other similar areas as in tropical Africa.

Chapter Eight

THE ACHIEVEMENT OF
ADULT STATUS

IT may now be possible to take stock of tropical Africa as it has developed since independence, and to try to see the position as a whole. It is not easy for an outsider to understand how Africa has been evolving, and in what direction it is likely to change in the near future. If we look back to the eve of independence, and consider what was expected of Africa then, we can see more easily how it has been moving. And by noting how far reality has fulfilled or belied the various forecasts that were then made, we will also help to remind ourselves how difficult it is to discern more than part of the pattern in advance.

To many outsiders—what may loosely be called conservative opinion—this large part of the earth's surface appeared a few years ago to be too inexperienced in the arts of running a modern state to be entrusted with self-government. African colonies seemed so technologically backward, so poor in accumulated wealth and in exploitable resources, so beset by traditional tribal jealousies and by new personal rivalries. Surely, such people asked, to dissolve the European Empires by 1960 into a jigsaw of independent states, some with less than a million largely illiterate inhabitants, would lead to internal chaos and invite external aggression, and perhaps touch off a series of revolutions on the classic Marxist pattern? When the Latin American countries acquired their independence a century and half ago, power passed into the hands of an

THE ACHIEVEMENT OF ADULT STATUS

educated white or mixed ruling class capable of conducting affairs of state. The Asian countries which came under colonial rule were the heirs of ancient and highly developed civilizations with solid traditions of literacy and government, and usually inherited a competent and Western-trained bureaucracy and managerial class too. The North African countries (except Algeria) were long-established kingdoms with the great Arabic tradition behind them. Even so, the successor states of the European Empires in those areas had not, in the eyes of these conservatives, managed their affairs very well. Did not the tropical African countries lack even these traditions and these ancient civilizations? Where were their administrative and managerial cadres? Did they not either lack, or propose to exclude from power, the largely white ruling class that took over the helm in Latin America? And finally, were not African societies still largely tribal, inchoate, not yet coagulated into nations? How could the new states be expected to stand up to the internal and external stresses that would inevitably beset them?

What may be called official and moderate opinion in the Western world (and here we must exclude Portugal) took it seems to me a more sanguine view. Africans were showing themselves to be politically quite competent: certainly in comparison with some other ex-colonial peoples. In any case they were growing steadily more politically impatient. A fairly rapid devolution of power by stages, at least towards self-government within some imperial system, seemed less likely to lead to bloodshed and to the destruction of property and trade, less likely to damage the achievements of trusteeship or the *mission civilisatrice* than an attempt to retain control by force for purposes which were becoming more nebulous in Western minds. Nor need self-government, or even independence, mean a radical break. Economic and perhaps political ties might survive in a *Communauté* or a Commonwealth, based on mutual consent and advantage. The new countries would continue to look largely to the former colonial power for trade, finance and expert personnel: perhaps, as non-colonial opinion of this kind hoped, drawing rather more on other Western powers as well. And surely the new African countries, whose cultural and state traditions were so much less established than those of Asia, would retain the language and practices of the colonial power, and with luck the carefully balanced institutions set up for them at the last stage of colonial rule?

More liberal and progressive opinion in the West, as we have seen, shared with the Marxists a dislike of colonialism. The establishment of European authority in tropical Africa, such people believed, had been a cynical scramble in the first place. Colonial rule was essentially oppressive and contrary to the best Western tradition of freedom and equality. Its basic motives were economic exploitation and strategic advantage. They were disturbed, and sometimes conscience-stricken, by the continuing poverty, ignorance and disease of Africa. In more sympathetic contact with the discontented élite of Africa than other Westerners, they accepted their anti-colonial convictions. But surely colonialism had also made easier the spread of liberal Western ideas? Were not the Westernized Africans who were now coming to power in their own countries imbued with a desire for liberty, equality, fraternity, or for the less precise but equally precious freedoms distilled by the Anglo-Saxon tradition? Were not these ideals the source of their African friends' longing for Freedom? And furthermore, had not many African leaders also adopted the progressive Western concepts of social justice and the welfare state? Progressive opinion hoped that, with aid and encouragement some at least of the African countries might move, in spite of the enormous difficulties, towards the free and progressive societies about which African leaders spoke.

I have outlined these three types of opinion in the West because each seems to me to point to certain aspects of the truth, as well as to certain errors which were largely subjective and which the unfolding of events is already begining to dispel. I have not tried to formulate opinion in Communist circles concerned with Africa. This is partly because it is so difficult to learn what this opinion really was in the period preceding independence, though the party propaganda line is familiar enough; and partly also because the Soviet and Chinese worlds were then, and still are, remote from tropical Africa. The awkwardness and lack of success of Communist operations there have been largely due to their ignorance and to their un-familiarity with the African scene, which is notoriously and elusively different from *a priori* suppositions of strangers.

Let us now look at what has actually happened in the new Africa. One of its first and most striking character-istics is its comparative stability, the internal order and authority, the relative rarity of armed aggression or sub-version directed by one new African state against another. (The great exception is the Congo, which is discussed below.) In this respect the fears of the conservatives have so far apparently been belied, though it is still too early to be sure; and official opinion justified. Moreover, official opinion was right in foreseeing that a major ingredient in this stability would be the continuing connexions of the new states after independence with the former colonial power and its close Western partners. The range and quantity of expertise and aid provided by the West on which the new countries can draw has helped to underpin the new regimes in the transitional period after the hand-over of power. This is particularly true of some of the smaller French states, which in many fields still continue to be administered largely with personnel and funds from the same sources as before independence. But, for all the invaluable help provided from without, the real basis of stability is the new African political system, the dominant and all-embracing national party. This single party system was forged in the struggle for independence and animated by the anti-colonialism which the Western progressives understood. But it could not hold to their liberal values; or to the balanced and circumscribed democracies evolved for the new states by the departing colonial powers, and in which official opinion placed some hopes. It is an African system: displeasing to many Westerners and owing less to their precepts and practices than they had hoped; but answering Africa's first need, the need that was used to justify the colonial occupation in the first place, the need for order.

Here I should say a short word about the Congo. It is not necessary to enter into the details of that country's tangled and exceedingly controversial history since independence in order to see that it is an outstanding exception to the orderliness with which independence has so far come to tropical Africa. The Congo is not markedly more ethnically complex than some more stable African countries. Nor are its technical problems markedly greater. Its sheer territorial extent, though enormous, does not appear to be the main difficulty. The essential handicap which beset the Congo was surely the abruptness of the transition from a country centrally and paternally administered to an independent state. There was not time before independence for the African system of a powerful and monolithic political machine to take hold and instal itself in power: neither one party throughout the country; nor an alliance of regional parties in effective control, as in Nigeria; nor a number of provincial parties each firmly installed in local administration of an area and so capable of maintaining order in a number of smaller states, as in French Equatorial Africa across the river. Recent experience suggests the maxim that handing over power to European-devised institutions will not ensure stability: there must be an African government in office with an authority of its own.

Another notable characteristic of tropical Africa since independence is the preoccupation of almost all its governments with the intractable problems of technical and economic backwardness and dependence. Western conservative opinion was right to stress how frighteningly large the problem is and how ill-equipped African countries are to meet it. Though awareness of this huge and growing gap is limited to a few leaders, their sense of it is one of the encouraging features of the scene since independence. It ensures that their desire for independence does not prevent even the most radical and anti-colonial of them from taking a great deal of the help which is offered, even while scrutinizing each offer from either East or West as if it were a wooden horse with neocolonialists in its belly. Indeed it is this desire for independence, and the resolve to translate political independence into an economic reality too, that usually impels African leaders to accept aid from the former colonial master and to ask for more, to retain many of the key colonial personnel and even to invite back some who had left (as happened in the Congo). Western progressives foresaw that aid would be treated as a means to independence more clearly than official opinion which tended to put too much trust in Africans wanting to maintain the colonial connexion for its own sake, as a few African leaders of course personally do. Generally speaking, Africans urgently want to stand on their own feet, and after the subjection of the colonial period to be beholden to nobody. The wiser among them, and this includes a large proportion of the leaders who have tried to grapple with the problem, realize that they cannot do so yet. And so, relatively secure in the authority which their political system gives them, they concentrate perhaps more objectively than many of their opposite numbers in the smaller countries of Asia and Latin America, on using what they can get from outside in order to bring the cadres, the economy and the technical resources of their countries to something approaching independence.

There can be no need to emphasize any further a third familiar characteristic: the general desire for independence in Africa. Nobody now supposes that this is an aspiration confined to a few "agitators", or politicians, or disgruntled tribes; and that the majority preferred the just and benevolent authority of a colonial administration. But it is perhaps important to note that moderate and official opinion (though not some well-placed officials), and many progressives too, were inclined to think or to hope that this desire would be satisfied by self-government. It is still easy to underestimate, unless one has experienced it at close quarters, the determination to be African, not just politically but in other ways too. The longing to be done with dependence, to cease being bound to Europe and its quarrels, to be neutral, to be themselves again, is often obscured by expediency, but remains in being. It is too much to say that colonial rule was a humiliation for Africans. For many it brought personal liberation and opportunity. But certainly, and at the least, colonialism was a school from which any sensitive person would be glad to graduate. Few Africans today have any desire to turn their backs on the modern world after passing through this school. Some would like to restore or maintain certain ancient tribal ways; but almost all those in positions of authority are eager enough for the power and the amenities which modern technology offers. And naturally they want to use these advantages in their own African way. We must not expect the new countries to reflect for very long the image of Britain or France. Already it is beginning to fade. The externals may survive awhile, especially in the former French territories. But underneath, African values and purposes will continue to assert themselves. In this context of the re-emergence of tropical Africa from colonial rule, it is useful to bear in mind the brevity of the colonial experience, for all its traumatic effectiveness.

In other words, the liquidation of the colonial system is usually a slow and gradual process of disentanglement. There are as we have seen great advantages in a long period of weaning, with the process of separation continuing on both sides of the attainment of political sovereignty. This is particularly true in the technical and economic fields. "Independence Day", the formal transfer of sovereignty, is the decisive step on the road from colonial subordination to nationhood, but it is certainly not the last. The new countries that are weaning themselves most gradually after independence are the four states of former French Equatorial Africa, which still lean heavily on France for the subsidies, the administrators and technicians, the protection from enemies and the assured markets that we associate with colonialism. Much that is typical of colonial times will doubtless continue there in slowly diminishing degrees for many years to come. At the other end of the scale, the Congo across the river found the breach with Belgium and the transition to a fairly absolute independence too sudden. After a period of confusion, the Congolese Government has had to turn to the United Nations and the United States and to renew some broken links with Belgium, in order to obtain similar (perhaps I may call them) post-independent colonial services as the ex-French states to the north continue to obtain from France. The example of Guinea is also instructive. When that country obtained its independence from France in 1958, and French aid and other services were cut off, it found itself unable to stand on its own feet—that is, to manage without substantial outside help. After canvassing France's allies, President Sékou Touré turned to the Soviet bloc. But he has apparently found the same difficulties in dealing with the Soviets as he feared from dependence on France. His *deux non*, first to Paris and then to Moscow, illustrate his resolve not to be unduly dependent on any one power in the process of taking the aid he needs to achieve a gradual evolution from sovereignty to genuine independence.

If this is the position, we must be careful about what is meant by saying that the sense of nationhood and of an independent personality in the new African countries conflicts with their economic and technical dependence and their need for continuing massive aid from outside. In a sense it is a real enough dilemma. If you must ensure a continuing flow of help of many diverse kinds, you cannot afford to express your personality as you please. You must trim your sails to a course which your donors will accept. And if your principal donor is the very colonial power whom you were compelled to obey before independence, both you and he will have to exercise restraint if a conflict is to be avoided. But at another level it is precisely this sense of nationhood and independent personality, combined with a sense of technical inadequacy, which impels African governments to take what aid they can get; and to spend what often amounts to a strikingly large proportion of it, not on consumption but on things which will help the new state to manage on its own. If there were not this striving towards independent nationhood, the need for aid—and especially aid invested to transform and diversify the economy—would be much less. *Les Sénégalais ne sont pas francophiles: mais fricophiles*, runs the saying. And though many Senegalese are fond of France and her civilization, it is true that what the new Republic wants from France is her *fric*.[1] And an encouraging amount of the aid received from France and elsewhere goes into nation-building: even in Senegal, which is not the African government most bent on emanci-

[1] Money

pating itself from colonialism and expressing its African personality.

If we accept that all the new countries of Africa are moving, in their own manner and by different routes, towards much the same goals, what is the best criterion for distinguishing them one from another? At one time it seemed to outside observers, and to many Africans too, that they could be divided into moderates and radicals: into the Monrovia and Casablanca groups, for instance, which they themselves had constituted. This distinction had a real validity; but the groupings have now lost much of their importance, and the categories seem inadequate. Official and moderate opinion still inclines to class countries as ex-British, ex-French and so on, making the distinction between radicals and moderates within these categories. So far as administrative matters are concerned, this categorization is obviously valid. Indeed the different colonial legacies penetrate deeper than this, into the very essence of the new states. But the conservatives and the progressives seem to be right when they say that it soon ceases to matter so much what imperial system a country once belonged to. We no longer group the countries of the Arab world, or South-East Asia, primarily according to their colonial past. And other distinctions, such as between democracies and dictatorships, or Islamic and non-Islamic states, are also inadequate by themselves, though they may point to important differences.

The most useful yardstick, to my mind, is the pace at which these countries are moving away from a colonial condition to adult status as genuinely independent nations. This is the issue that most interests Africans; and as a country progresses towards this goal so it moves into a new context, in which the distinctions and categories of the immediate post-independence period listed in the last paragraph come to matter less.

This pace of advance is not to be measured, of course, simply by putting at the head of the list those countries which made the most radical breach with the colonial power, or swung most heavily towards state socialism and government control. It is not the Monrovia-Casablanca division in disguise. Guinea's overhastiness yesterday, or Kenya's tomorrow, could slow down the pace of their advance. Nigeria, a leader of the "moderate" group, is moving steadily towards an adult and genuine independence, and devoting major efforts to equipping herself for the task. Even if President Houphouet loses his bet with President Nkrumah about who will attain the most prosperous and developed economy, both may find themselves ahead of many others in the pace of their advance.

In using this yardstick we must also be careful not to confuse it with technological progress. Rapid technical advance does not seem to all Africans the highest good. Even its social aspects, the struggles against hunger, against illiteracy, against disease, which seem to Westerners such human and necessary goals, are in Africa means to an end. They rank with the campaign for industrialization and improved agricultural techniques, as part of the great objective of building new, free, African nations: of ending their client status and taking their places as adult and respected members of world society. Until this position has been achieved, those who have been humiliated by the lack of it will not easily turn their minds to other objectives. So we cannot measure the advance that interests Africans merely by technical standards either. On many such tests, as Africans frequently point out, areas of white settlement come out high. However useful these technical assets may prove when it comes to nation-building in the future, so long as such countries are not under African control the essential element is lacking.

Of course there are differences and arguments, both among Africans and others, about what constitutes a real advance in this process of nation-building. A balance between many elements, without extreme concentration on any one of them, seems to be most successful. African-ism, and disentanglement from Europe, must be weighed against material progress; though some claim that the two are not opposites and can be combined. Certainly to build a new nation requires a degree of popular enthusiasm and of perseverence. People can be discouraged by too much dragooning and compulsion in the name of pro-gress; but apathy and frustration can equally be caused by a government which shows itself indifferent to popular welfare and to the continent-wide striving towards a more genuine independence. There must also be a con-siderable degree of economic achievement: if possible yielding increased rewards both now, in order to meet or partly meet people's rising expectations, and in the future to further the cause of economic emancipation. Again, coercion and the severance of traditional economic links can lead to something like economic paralysis, as at one time it seemed to be doing in Guinea; but Guinea's supporters retort that graft and complaisance, and the continuation of the colonial economy, can also cause the economy to stagnate, as more than one example in Africa shows. Furthermore, while the judgement of the citizens must be a main criterion of success, it is not the only one.

The opinion of other Africans counts for much; as does the esteem of the outside world. The states which have won good opinions from outside have usually been moderate ones, "midway between rage and sloth". But among wide circles of Africans, and especially the young and the educated, radicalism has an appeal which conservatism has not. Where so very much needs to be done, going too fast may be as dangerous as going too slow, but to many Africans it seems more forgiveable.

A final characteristic of the new African states which we may note, and which differs from what outside observers and perhaps most Africans expected, is their relation to each other. On many issues, as we have seen in Chapter Seven, and more particularly on those which affect Africans as a whole there is solidarity. This sense of unity, one might say of community, seems to be stronger than that which unites either the Latin Americans or the Arabs, despite their closer ties of language and culture. But like the other two groups, the African union has so far been one of nation states: some unitary and some federal, but almost without exception determined not to submerge the national entities they are building in a wider Pan-African government.

The conservatives have been proved right in stressing the lack of long-standing national sentiment in most African territories, and the pull of narrower loyalties such as the tribe as well as the wider ones of Pan-Africa. The progressives were perhaps inclined to listen too much to those Africans who dreamed of a militant and more or less Marxist Union of African States (were they wrong, or could it possibly still be round the corner?). It was the officials and moderates, particularly in France, who understood that the territories delineated by the colonial powers for their administrative convenience had acquired an African life and vitality of their own, and realized that almost all of them would wish and be able to maintain a vigorous existence, either as independent nations or as consciously autonomous members of a federation. Neither tribalism nor Pan-Africanism has led, as conservatives feared they might, to any serious violation of the boundaries established in colonial times.

In general, we may conclude that when we in the West think about Africa, we must decolonize the image of it in our minds, so to speak, in order to keep pace with the progressive reassertion of independence in Africa itself. This is especially true for those of us who are citizens of the former colonial powers; but the need also exists elsewhere. The first step is to accept the independence of these countries and to recognize that it will confirm itself and grow stronger with time. Most of us have taken this step: some with regret, and others with satisfaction.

The next stage will probably be for us to feel less possessive, less concerned over what the new governments there do, less (it has been aptly said) like a governess at a children's party, anxious that her own charges should reflect credit on themselves and on her who brought them up. This possessiveness and concern has its advantages for Africans while its lasts, of course. No doubt it ensures them a greater flow of aid than they would otherwise be able to count on, for instance; and other useful things like sponsorship in international negotiations. But the reaction in the ex-imperial countries is the sharper when "their" Africans stray from the ways they consider seemly or wise. People in Britain do not yet regard the internal affairs of, say, Ghana or Uganda in the same detached way as they do events in countries like Pakistan or Egypt. It is notoriously difficult to make predictions about an area so new and unpredetermined as independent Africa. But it seems likely that with the passage of time, whether for better or for worse, Englishmen will feel no more implicated in the African countries they once administered, or responsible for them, than they do for other states over which they formerly ruled for much longer periods. In time too, no doubt, the French people will come for the same reasons to feel no more responsible for the Cameroons than for Syria. This change will carry with it a corresponding decline in our sense of special obligation towards these countries, as they come to stand increasingly on their own feet. Aid by highly developed countries to less developed ones seems likely to continue. But it has already begun to assume more diffused and less "national" forms. Will this tendency become more marked as time goes on?

Implicit in this growing detachment is a third evolution of thinking about Africa, which has perhaps gone further in Africa itself and in countries like the United States than in Europe. It is to look on tropical Africa as a whole, as a quite closely knit area of the world, like the Arab lands or Latin America, whose different governments and peoples have much in common and are often prepared to act in concert when they see their common interests affected. This image may become clearer for the outside world if the tentative moves so far taken by African leaders towards forming a Union of African states continue, so that an effective and meaningful political organization emerges. It is quite possible that much of Africa will come together in something more closely knit than the majority of African governments have so far been willing to accept: perhaps something of a confederal nature or on the lines of the proposed European Community. But in any case, even if no constitutional structure of this kind is evolved, or an agreement is reached which turns out to amount to little in practice, the African states will probably continue to develop the habit of consulting one another and co-ordinating their policies. As this comes about, so our way of thinking about the area will be modified to correspond with the new reality.

European observers, whatever their political sympathies, must wonder how far the evolution towards continental co-operation and potential union, which now seems likely in Africa, will affect the ties of certain countries with other members of their former "imperial family" including the "metropole". The answer would seem to be that, so long as these ties help the process of nation-building, and do not cut across the operation of the new continental African solidarity which is being forged, they are likely to survive. As political detachment from the former colonial power becomes an accepted reality, these ties may come to seem increasingly welcome.

Within any African framework which may grow up, it seems very probable that the French-speaking countries will remain, as they are now, in specially close touch among themselves. The bonds of a common language and tradition, the long-standing personal acquaintance among their leaders, and continuing economic and other ties will hold them together. And links of the same sort, along with French aid and advice, will similarly keep their links of interest and affection to France alive. The English-speaking countries are more divergent from each other: partly because British colonialism did not set out to assimilate the élite which is now in power, and provided the territories with less uniform administrative systems. But their decision to stand aside from association with the European Economic Community, if maintained, will in the next few years no doubt also help to bring them together.

This is not the place to speculate about the future evolution of the multi-racial, multi-continental Commonwealth. For the near future, the significant links of the African members of the Commonwealth are likely to be with each other and with Britain, rather than with the Commonwealth as a whole. But the sense of a common language, experience and ways of doing things, which gives these links their strength, also makes it easier for the new African members of that body to cooperate with similar countries in other continents too. Economic and technical advantages, too, tend to flow more easily along Commonwealth channels. Such contacts will not of themselves make the new African members of the Commonwealth less African. There does not seem to be any obvious reason why ties of the kind that, for example, India now maintains and values with other members of the Commonwealth need conflict with the role which members of the Commonwealth in Africa will wish to play in the affairs of that continent in the coming years.

If federal institutions covering all or much of tropical Africa are eventually set up, and the present sovereign countries become provinces of what for international purposes is recognized as a single government, a number of major constitutional questions will arise. But although a number of African leaders, including President Nkrumah, are working to this end, and the constitutions of more than one African state make provision for the surrender of sovereignty for this purpose, it is as we have seen unlikely to be realized in the near future. Even so, the mere fact that it is on the political agenda between the African states illustrates the need to think of tropical Africa as an area with common aspirations and problems, rather than as separate collections of ex-colonial lands.

Chapter Nine

THE PLACE OF THE NEW AFRICAN
STATES IN THE WORLD

IN this final chapter I propose by way of a conclusion to see what can usefully be said about the position which the outside world is likely to accord to the new Africa: and in particular about the future course of relations between it and the West.

Africans and people interested in Africa must beware of exaggerating the importance of the tropical zone of the continent in the global scheme of things. During the present period, when it is reasserting its independence, or if you prefer while the colonial powers are relinquishing their authority, Africa is much in the news, and attracts a good deal of the outside world's attention. But this is by its nature a transitory phenomenon. If the record so far proves a reliable guide, and the great majority of the new countries do not slide into chaos after external authority has been removed but manage to maintain secure and orderly government, a new and calmer context will establish itself. But we are not there yet. In some critical parts of Africa, notably the Portuguese territories and at the time of writing the Congo and Southern Rhodesia, external authority has not yet been removed, and the capacities of independent African authority remain to be demonstrated. Personal memories, the struggle to complete the liberation of the continent, and fears of neo-colonialism, still cause the ghost of the colonial relationship to haunt the new African states for some time after the reality has died. So far as the West is concerned, a more objective appraisal, by Africans of Europe and by the Western powers of independent Africa, will doubtless have to wait at least until the emancipation of Africa from overseas rule has been completed.

South Africa is a different case. The three million or so white men there are regarded by Africans as alien intruders. Their supremacy is coming to be increasingly resented throughout the continent. But they are certainly not the agents of overseas imperialism. Are they in this respect perhaps to be compared to Israel, also a settlement of more technically advanced aliens in the Arab world? Certainly there would be a parallel if the white population withdrew to a part of the present Republic, and within these new limits constituted an overwhelming majority. The new relationship between the Arab states and the Western powers, that has gradually been establishing itself since virtually all the Arab countries have attained their political independence, is complicated but not fundamentally altered by the existence of Israel. Shall we find that whatever solution is reached in South Africa (where the white population is hardly likely to be expelled), it will similarly not prevent the growth of less emotional and more objective attitudes between the new Africa and the West? In fact, France's relations with Africa are scarcely affected by the South African issue even now: the complicating factor in her case was—and perhaps still is—Algeria.

We may take it as fairly certain, therefore, that relations between Africa and the West will continue to change fairly rapidly. Is it possible at this early stage to discern their future shape?

Perhaps we may start by asking what the West wants from Africa. What sort of conditions does it wish to see there? And what sort of effort is it willing to make, what price will it pay, to ensure that these conditions prevail? We can then match these Western purposes against what we know of African aims, and so try to see what types of bargain are likely to be struck.

Two traditional Western interests in Africa, the strategic and the economic, seem likely to decline in importance. Let us take the strategic problem first. Rivalry between the powers of Western Europe was certainly one of the main reasons for the partition of Africa; and for a time this rivalry, the existence of far-flung empires and the nature of warfare made Africa an area of considerable strategic importance. But today active rivalry between the Western powers has evaporated, and their empires have disappeared. Methods of waging war, and of bringing force to bear, are changing rapidly. Concern in the West about strategic bases, overflying rights and access to vital raw materials is diminishing: not only in Africa but all round the world. This is part of a general trend in strategy. As the disentanglement of Africa from Europe continues, as the current evidence indicates that it will, and as more dispassionate views begin to prevail, so we may expect the West to attach less importance to its strategic interests in that continent. It is not sour grapes when the Western powers say they no longer really need the bases and facilities that Africans are now more reluctant to concede.

Western strategic facilities in tropical Africa will not all be given up at once, of course. Inertia and the cost of building alternative installations often produce a lingering reluctance to abandon dispositions for defence. But certainly many of the West's remaining strongpoints in Africa are becoming anachronistic enough to be irrelevant to contemporary requirements. Who supposes that Britain, France and Belgium by giving up their African colonies have become less able to contribute to the defence of the West? Was not a major reason for France getting out of Algeria that she did not want to tie down so much military capacity in that area?

For some time, in short, it has been clear that the European powers (always with the exception of Portugal) have decided that it is not expedient to maintain by force their special position in the areas of Africa which they chalked out for themselves in the 1880s and occupied during the following two decades. They seem to be coming to the further conclusion that such special interests are hardly worth paying much of a price for in any case. And so, as we saw in the first two chapters of this book, the West is likely in its dealings with Africa to revert to the more generalized relations that existed before the great partition. Commitments and interests built up over the colonial era will not disappear. The West will not turn its back on Africa; any more than Africa, introduced by the West to modern civilization, and imbued with Western culture, Western languages and Western ways of doing things, will turn its back on the West. But—and this is a tautology that needs repeating— relations between the two will become less colonial as the eighty years of effective colonialism recede into the past.

We may expect the West, then, gradually to relinquish all positive strategic facilities, and acquiesce in a substantially neutral and indeed neutralist policy by the new

African states. But the Western powers will probably not take kindly to their enemies gaining a predominant position there. They will not want the Communist powers to step into the position which the Western governments are relinquishing. What this objection will mean in practice it is difficult to see. Who can forecast the future course of the West's relations with Russia, for example? An Oxford political philosopher, Professor Plamenatz, has formulated the case for less Western concern about Russian activities in Africa even now. "The Western Powers are too prone to act as if any advance made towards Russia, or any help received from her, by an Asian or African people were a victory for Communism. To receive help from Moscow is not necessarily to be in Moscow's clutches. Especially it is not so if there is also help to be got from other sources. . . . If we are willing to give help to backward countries unconditionally in the hope that this will prevent their falling into Communist hands, why should Moscow not be willing to do the same to prevent their falling too much under our influence?" Opinions will differ about the wisdom of this course; and these opinions will be coloured by differing estimates not only of Soviet intentions but also of the value to the West of denying Russia a substantial position in tropical Africa.

The economic importance of tropical Africa to the West is also likely to decline further in Western eyes. Here too general ideas are changing. One of the justifications of colonial empire to doubters at home used to be that it assured markets and sources of supply. But when underdeveloped countries become independent, their new governments are most anxious to sell what they can produce; and the advanced economies that buy these products are in a good position to sell in return what the new countries desperately need. There is also less enthusiam in the West today than there used to be for tariff privileges, quotas and guaranteed markets. Moreover, Western economic policy will increasingly be determined by powers with no significant ex-colonial attachments.

In any case tropical Africa produces little, if anything, that the West really needs, or could not with a little time, difficulty and extra cost obtain very well elsewhere. Certainly not the cotton, the coffee and tea, the tobacco, the vegetable oils on which so many of the new countries largely depend for exports. One has only to mention these commodities to see what a buyer's market they are likely to remain. A few commodities like cocoa may be in better case. Of the minerals, iron ore may prove to be the most useful asset. The world would not find it very difficult to manage without African copper or aluminium. Such an imaginary interruption would entail losses for certain interests and companies in the West, and even for certain countries; but it would mean a disaster for Africa without seriously damaging the West. More significant is the impact of the marginal choices exercised by Western importers and consumers: which may make a major difference to the external purchasing power and so to the rate of development of African countries without seriously rippling the surface of Western life. And what prospects can be held out to African countries of marketing in the West the new and diversified products which they hope not only to substitute for imports but also if possible to sell abroad?

It is in this context of decreasing Western interest that the African countries will be struggling to decolonialize their economies, and to lessen their economic dependence on their former imperial masters. Clearly this process, as it succeeds, must be expected to lessen still further the sense of responsibility and possessiveness even of Britain and France towards their former territories. Concepts like "Eurafrica", in the sense of treating tropical Africa as a kind of extension of Europe and granting it special facilities in European markets, will be likely to fade. There will be a new economic nexus between Africa and the West.

The most positive requirement the West will have in Africa—what it really will want to see there—is capable self-government. That is: the maintenance of law and order; security for trade and industry and for the foreigners who work in the new countries on the terms laid down by the African governments; and reasonable respect for the international obligations which these governments accept. This is what Europeans wanted, and did not always find, in pre-colonial Africa. It is fortunately something that most African governments today seem able to provide.

Western commercial enterprises with existing investments in an African country—and this involves everything from money to goodwill—will want to foster these conditions if they can. They will, as they did before the colonial occupation, urge Western governments to use their influence to help maintain and improve such conditions. And it is a truism that private enterprises will not put fresh capital into a newly independent country in return for moderate gain unless they consider that the country and the regime have good prospects for maintaining order and stability for some years to come.

Business men have learnt by experience that the prospects of stability in fluid and rapidly changing conditions are best ensured, not by a rigidly conservative regime but by one capable of adapting its policies to meet the political and economic problems which might otherwise mount until they engulfed it. In other words, foreign private enterprise will look for orderly progress; both to safeguard existing commitments and as a prerequisite for bringing in more money and effort from outside. The weight of business influence, both directly through the private investment it is prepared to make and indirectly through the influence it can exert on Western and African governments, is shifting towards a policy of helping African countries to solve problems rather than sit on them. This policy is naturally always subject to the proviso that the solutions adopted do not seriously damage foreign investments, e.g. by taking over assets with manifestly unreasonable compensation. But ideas of what is reasonable in this field also seem to be changing.

At the present stage the views of the business communities of the West are not only important because of their large existing role in the trade and development of Africa. Almost all the new African governments rely on foreign private enterprise to play its part in the major aid and development schemes which they work out with Western governments and international bodies like the World Bank (the International Bank for Reconstruction and Development, which exists precisely in order to facilitate such participation). Most of the new governments also hope that foreign enterprise will supplement these large and government-sponsored schemes with smaller-scale development and expansion projects which may or may not require the active collaboration of the African government concerned. The economic planning of most African governments is predicated on the assumption that foreign private enterprise will be forthcoming in considerable volume under both these heads. Even the more radical states like Guinea and Ghana assign a significant place to private foreign enterprise in their plans. One of the worrying aspects of African development over the next few years is that these assumptions may well turn out to have been too optimistic, and that foreign private capital will not in fact flow into Africa in anything like the quantities required.

Western governments, in a post-imperialist and decolonizing mood, are (notwithstanding allegations to the contrary) reluctant to intervene in African affairs, inclined to mistrust intervention as likely to do more harm than good, and unlikely to do so if they can help it. But they are naturally anxious to protect and encourage their nationals' economic enterprises. This is why one major purpose of the aid they give is, as we have seen, to help African governments maintain order and economic prosperity in their countries, and also to ensure that those governments have at their disposal the means of solving their most pressing political and social problems.

If governments of a more socialist persuasion come to power in some of the leading Western countries, they may be guided in formulating their policies for aid to Africa less by the need to foster and protect enlightened forms of private enterprise, and more by the other motives for giving aid listed in Chapter Five. But this will only be a difference of degree, a minor shift in the broad pattern of the West's economic relationship with Africa in the next few years.

Will the West go further than this, and try to persuade Africans of the value of democratic liberties, Western concepts of society and Western ethics? We have looked at the reasons for thinking that Western governments will probably not do so. They will be satisfied to see Africans governing effectively and capably; and making a reasonable and not too wasteful use of the aid accepted from the West. It does not seem probable that Western governments will give substantially more aid to African governments markedly friendly to the West. They will not, that is to say, pay a substantial premium for pro-Western attitudes and behaviour. But an element of this preference there is bound to be. And certainly Western governments and peoples will not, once colonial issues are out of the way in Africa, be willing to reward active hostility to the West and its interests in the same way as friendship and co-operation.

It is rather non-governmental institutions, and the whole wide network of private and personal contacts between Westerners and Africans, which will be used to argue with Africans the value of Western ways. This is natural and desirable enough. It is scarcely possible for a man who holds certain civic and social values strongly not to urge them on his friends. But more Westerners, used to the give and take of such discussions among themselves, realize that there are limits to the extent you can persuade people with other traditions and beliefs to see the objective advantages of your values. The Westerners who are best placed to do this are not visitors, but those experts

who work in the educational systems of the new countries, and in other advisory and technical capacities. Many
of these experts are ready enough to expound and urge
the merits of Western ways. But because their task is to
make an African system work, they are also anxious to
ensure that what is adopted from the West should be
properly integrated into African society and serve those
needs which are most pressing in Africa today. And they
are coming increasingly to remind visitors that, as might
be expected, sixty years of colonialism have not Westernized Africa as profoundly as is sometimes imagined.

We have seen that as African governments re-establish
their continent's independence, and as the West ceases to
be responsible for them, they are thus likely to discover
that their economic relations with the West will not be
adequate for them to develop as fast or as diversely as they
now hope and plan to do. Even when all the great volume
of Western aid is taken into account, the new countries
will not be able to offer the West enough, and will not
matter enough to the West, to obtain from it all that they
need. And in any case for deeper political reasons they
will not be prepared to limit themselves to the position
of clients of the Western world, but will want to look
further afield.

In this situation economic relations with the Soviet
bloc seem fairly certain to increase. Though the more
radical governments have learnt, sometimes by experience, the dangers of slipping into a state of economic
dependence on the Communist system, they are likely to
maintain and perhaps expand the profitable exchanges,
often with a quite high aid content, that they find themselves able to arrange. The more moderate governments

too are well aware of the potential market in the Eastern bloc for specialized tropical products and raw materials, as consumption rises there. President Houphouet Boigny is as anxious to sell Ivory Coast coffee in Russia as President Nkrumah is to sell Ghanaian cocoa. Scholarships and other forms of aid are also likely to be increasingly accepted.

But the economic and other advantages offered by the Soviet bloc are limited (the market is not indefinitely expandible and African countries will have to compete for it with other tropical areas). And to many Africans they seem much more like the advantages offered by the West than Westerners suppose. The Soviet countries too have highly developed and technically advanced societies: with somewhat different forms of organization and unfamiliar languages, no doubt, but with similar requirements and facilities. Like the West they can absorb specialized products in fair quantities, and they can teach. But African governments are having to ask themselves whether it is realistic to assume that either the West alone, or even the developed world taken as a whole, will absorb the greatly increased production for which their plans provide.

As it becomes clear to Africans in positions of responsibility that neither the West nor the Soviet bloc are likely to consume much greater quantities of specialized African products, or indeed large quantities of basic foodstuffs like cereals and meat which Africa could probably produce, some Africans and their foreign economic advisers are beginning to look further afield. It may be—though this is still a new thought in Africa—that only the hungry millions of Asia offer a potential market for the greatly expanded production of foodstuffs and other raw materials on which African countries must rely to pay even partly for the economic transformation they are determined to achieve. How far could Asian countries like India supply capital goods and technical expertise in return? Certainly they could supply Africa's other great need, low-cost consumer goods of almost every kind.

Few Africans have yet formulated any clear ideas about what could be done in these fields. To find the answers is one of the forms of help which they need: and most of them expect such help and advice to come mainly from the West. Well-informed Africans realize that such arrangements would no doubt go beyond what private enterprise in the outside world would find it profitable to organize unaided. New markets and sources of supply in Asia may nevertheless have to be arranged over and above what the West is prepared to do directly, if many of the new African countries are not to sink slowly into increasing discontent as their economic standards of living fall further behind both their own expectations and the standard of development and welfare realized in the more advanced countries. Some observers see here a real Western interest, because it is in the risk of decline and discontent that they consider the real threat to Western interests in Africa to lie.

I have tried to describe in this book the background against which the newly established independent states of tropical Africa operate, and the problems with which their governments must contend in their task of building stable new nations. These problems are great, but not overwhelming. The natural deficiencies of tropical Africa are serious enough. But most of them can be overcome;

and carry with them their own compensations meanwhile. The area is comparatively poor in natural resources. But on the whole the new countries established there are not overpopulated, like many Asian ones. Their people do not suffer in the same way from acute poverty, hunger and disease. On balance the resources of the land are still underexploited rather than used up or eroded. Again, Africans are still for the most part technically backward, and lack the skills of the West or Asia. There is little accumulated wealth. But education is beginning to alter this picture. Meanwhile social evolution is not effectively blocked by rigid class and caste structures and by the accumulation of great wealth in a few hands. If the outside world maintains its present willingness to help, there is a fair prospect of tropical Africa progressing from the present decisive resumption of its international sovereignty to the realization of administrative, economic and spiritual independence. And there are grounds for hope that most of the new nations will manage to achieve this goal in conditions of internal order and stability, of external co-operation with their neighbours, and of reasonable respect for the international obligations they assume. Of course there will be disappointments and exceptions. These are high standards. But tropical Africa seems likely to measure up to them quite as well as other comparable areas like the Arab world, South-East Asia or Central America and the Caribbean. And it is encouraging that to most observers the prospect seems better today than it did, say, five years ago.

In their efforts to bring their countries forward, the governments and peoples of tropical Africa have some claim to the sympathy and to the detachment of the

West. They have a claim to sympathy because the Western world, and particularly Britain and France, have played a large part in bringing them to their present position. It will be a harder task than most Africans imagined to make their new countries into modern communities, and to emancipate them both from the technological backwardness that has hitherto marked Africa, and also from the colonial or nearly colonial dependence on the advanced world that has been its inevitable corollary ever since the expansion of Europe forced modern technology on a continent that had been developing at a slower pace. To achieve this task, the Africans will need Western help, and the sympathy to ensure that it is forthcoming.

They are also entitled to our detachment, because the West has now agreed to let Africans resume the direction of their own affairs. The West should not expect to see a reflection of itself in the new Africa. For Africans are resolved to work out their separate destinies in their own way. Of course, like the rest of mankind, they will only partially succeed in realizing their aims. It seems to me that the West can help them, advise them, bargain with them. But the newly independent countries of tropical Africa are no longer the wards of the West; and the West is not responsible for what they decide to do.

APPENDIX A

Note on the French System of providing experts to Tropical African Countries formerly under French Rule

French aid to undeveloped countries is almost entirely concentrated on countries formerly administered by France. For various reasons the Asian ex-colonies receive little of this, and almost all of it goes to Africa. Aid to North Africa is in a special category.

The thirteen ex-French African countries now organized in the U.A.M. (*Union Africaine et Malgache*), together with Mali, receive French aid in a number of ways (not all of which apply to every country). These can be classified as:

(*a*) Budgetary subventions for current expenditure (not to the richer republics)

(*b*) Direct bilateral development

(*c*) Development aid from the generous French contribution to the Overseas Development Fund of E.E.C.

(*d*) Military aid and training

(*e*) Educational facilities in France and the maintenance in Africa, from French funds, of Universities and Higher Educational Institutes notably the University of Dakar

(*f*) The provision of technical and administrative personnel to the fourteen Republics (*g*) Assistance with schemes for training African personnel in Africa.

This note concerns category (*f*), that is the provision of technical and administrative personnel.

French aid to the U.A.M. states and Mali under this heading has two characteristics. Firstly, everything is centralized through the Ministry of Aid and Co-operation in Paris. Secondly, almost all the French personnel in these countries are provided largely free of charge to the new African states. French procedure is uniformly standardized for the U.A.M. Republics. There are minor differences in the case of Mali, but these do not affect the general picture.

The personnel provided by France to the African Republics are divided into two categories: technicians (most of whom are teachers), and administrators.

The technicians and teachers who were serving in the territories in question at the time of independence were absorbed hypothetically into the various appropriate French Ministries. These include the Ministry of Education; which in France is responsible for the teaching staff in state schools. This arrangement ensured continuity of career for the civil servants in question. Those who were prepared to continue to serve as French civil servants in the new African Republics, and whom the now independent governments wished to retain, were allowed to stay. These teachers were not on loan from their new parent Ministry, but were seconded by that Ministry to the Ministry of Co-operation, which was responsible for their administration and pay. The experts or technicians were then lent to the new independent governments; who made their own decisions on which to use in their former executive capacities and which to use as advisers or technical counsellors to African executive officers.

Administrative officers of the French Colonial Service, who did not fit so easily into existing French Ministries, were given the opportunity of returning to France for re-integration into a suitable branch of the Home Civil Service or the French Foreign Service. They could exercise this option either at the start of independence or later. These also were seconded by the French Ministry of Co-operation to individual governments to use either in an executive or an advisory capacity.

The African governments reimbursed to the French Government a proportion of the salary of each official borrowed in these two categories. The average sum re-imbursed by the governments of the twelve U.A.M. Republics amounts to 45,000 francs C.F.A. a month (about £1,300 a year). This is roughly one-fifth of the cost to the French taxpayer. It must be remembered that in the case of several Republics the sum so reimbursed comes from a French budget subvention, in the sense that budget subventions are designed to take into account the employment of French technicians.

The French Government pays its civil servants on loan to the tropical African Republics 60 per cent. more altogether (including allowances) than they would receive in equivalent grades in France itself. In addition they are entitled to two months' home leave for every ten months of service, with their transport and that of their wives and children paid by the French Government. While at their post they receive a rent free house, and sometimes utilities like electricity and water and even servants. Personnel seconded from France receive in local currency the salaries and allowances corresponding to the equivalent grades of African personnel employed by the governments in question. The balance is paid in France in order to avoid local jealousy. The 60 per cent. premium is often regarded as rather less than adequate by the seconded members of the French Colonial Service because the cost of living for Europeans in French tropical Africa is usually at least 60 per cent. more than in France.

At present there are about 14,000 technical, educational and administrative personnel of this kind in the U.A.M. states and Mali. The French Ministry of Co-operation estimated in 1962 that originally 17 per cent. of the personnel taken over at the time of independence were Africans; but now almost all of them are from metropolitan France. About half, or slightly more than 7,000 people, are connected with education. The most advanced of the Republics have always been willing to engage, and have been offered, the largest number of experts. The largest single figure is approximately 1,500 in Madagascar. Then come Senegal with 1,400 and the Ivory Coast with 1,300. There are about 500 such members of the French Colonial Service on loan to Mali. The totals for the least developed countries are about 400.

The French Government expects the number of teachers seconded to the African Republics to rise, and all other categories to decline. Monsieur Foyer, the former Minister of Co-operation, has said that the Ministry wishes to recruit about 1,000 more teachers a year for some three or four years and to allow a slightly smaller annual reduction in the other categories. These teachers are responsible for all the subjects in the curriculum, including the teaching of English and German.

The future of this considerable number of French experts depends on the success of the plans for training adequate African cadres. Thus, many of the African governments in question are only willing to accept such large numbers of French experts on the understanding that this is a temporary arrangement and that a progression of training Africans will be actively pursued with French money and help. The organization of such centres and the selection of suitable candidates has run into considerable difficulties. The Institute of Higher Overseas Studies in France and smaller training centres in certain of the African Republics have only begun to tackle the problem.

In each of the Republics in question the French Government maintains an Aid and Co-operation Mission, separated from the French Embassy (though often under the general jurisdiction of the Ambassador). These Missions are similar to the U.S. Aid Missions. They supervise and pay the personnel discussed in this note as well as concerning themselves with other forms of French aid.

The Charter of the Organization of African Unity

We, the Heads of African States and Governments assembled in the City of Addis Ababa, Ethiopia;

CONVINCED that it is the inalienable right of all people to control their own destiny;

CONSCIOUS of the fact that freedom, equality, justice and dignity are essential objectives for the achievement of the legitimate aspirations of the African peoples;

CONSCIOUS of our responsibility to harness the natural and human resources of our continent for the total advancement of our peoples in spheres of human endeavour;

INSPIRED by a common determination to strengthen understanding and co-operation among our States in response to the aspirations of our peoples for brotherhood and solidarity, in a larger unity transcending ethnic and national differences;

CONVINCED that, in order to translate this determination into a dynamic force in the cause of human progress, conditions for peace and security must be established and maintained;

DETERMINED to safeguard and consolidate the hard-won independence as well as the sovereignty and territorial integrity of our States, and to fight against neo-colonialism in all its forms;

DEDICATED to the general progress of Africa;

PERSUADED that the Charter of the United Nations and the Universal Declaration of Human Rights, to the principles of which we reaffirm our adherence, provide a solid foundation for peaceful and positive co-operation among States;

DESIROUS that all African States should henceforth unite so that the welfare and well-being of their peoples can be assured;

RESOLVED to reinforce the links between our States by establishing and strengthening common institutions;

HAVE agreed to the present Charter.

ESTABLISHMENT

ARTICLE I

1. The High Contracting Parties do by the present Charter establish an Organization to be known as the "Organization of AFRICAN UNITY".

2. The Organization shall include the Continental African States, Madagascar and all the islands surrounding Africa.

PURPOSES

ARTICLE II

1. The Organization shall have the following purposes:

(*a*) to promote the unity and solidarity of the African States;

(*b*) to co-ordinate and intensify their co-operation and efforts to achieve a better life for the peoples of Africa;

(*c*) to defend their sovereignty, their territorial integrity and independence;

(*d*) to eradicate all forms of colonialism from Africa; and (*e*) to promote international co-operation, having due regard to the Charter of the United Nations and the Universal Declaration of Human Rights.

2. To these ends, the Members State shall co-ordinate and harmonize their general policies, especially in the following fields:

(*s*) political and diplomatic co-operation;
(*b*) economic co-operation, including transport and communications;
(*c*) educational and cultural co-operation;
(*d*) health, sanitation, and nutritional co-operation;
(*e*) scientific and technical co-operation; and
(*f*) co-operation for defence and security.

PRINCIPLES

ARTICLE III

The Member States, in pursuit of the purposes stated in Article II, solemnly affirm and declare their adherence to the following principles:

(1) the sovereign equality of all Member States;
(2) non-interference in the internal affairs of States;
(3) respect for the sovereignty and territorial integrity of each Member State and for its inalienable right to independent existence;
(4) peaceful settlement of disputes by negotiations, mediation, conciliation or arbitration;
(5) unreserved condemnation, in all its forms, of political assassination as well as of subversive activities on the part of neighbouring States or any other States;

(6) absolute dedication to the total emancipation of the African territories which are still dependent;

(7) affirmation of a policy of non-alignment with regard to all blocs.

MEMBERSHIP

ARTICLE IV

Each independent sovereign African State shall be entitled to become a Member of the Organization.

RIGHTS AND DUTIES OF MEMBER STATES

ARTICLE V

All Member States shall enjoy equal rights and have equal duties.

ARTICLE VI

The Member States pledge themselves to observe scrupulously the principles enumerated in Article III of the present Charter.

INSTITUTIONS

ARTICLE VII

The Organization shall accomplish its purposes through the following principal institutions:

(1) the Assembly of Heads of State and Government;
(2) the Council of Ministers;
(3) the General Secretariat;
(4) the Commission of Mediation, Conciliation and Arbitration.

THE ASSEMBLY OF HEADS OF STATE AND GOVERNMENT

ARTICLE VIII

The Assembly of Heads of State and Government shall be the supreme organ of the Organization. It shall, subject to the provisions of this Charter, discuss matters of common concern to Africa with a view to co-ordinating and harmonizing the general policy of the Organization. It may in addition review the structure, functions and acts of all the organs and any specialized agencies which may be created in accordance with the present Charter.

ARTICLE IX

The Assembly shall be composed of the Heads of State, Government or their duly accredited representatives and it shall meet at least once a year. At the request of any Member State, and approval by the majority of the Member States, the Assembly shall meet in extraordinary Session.

ARTICLE X

1. Each Member State shall have one vote.
2. All resolutions shall be determined by a two-thirds majority of the Members of the Organization.
3. Questions of procedure shall require a simple majority. Whether or not a question is one of procedure shall be determined by a simple majority of all Member States of the Organization.
4. Two-thirds of the total membership of the Organization shall form a quorum at any meeting of the Assembly.

ARTICLE XI

The Assembly shall have the power to determine its own rules of procedure.

THE COUNCIL OF MINISTERS

ARTICLE XII

The Council of Ministers shall consist of Foreign Ministers or such other Ministers as are designated by the Governments of Member States.

The Council of Ministers shall meet at least twice a year. When requested by any Member State and approved by two-thirds of all Member States, it shall meet in extraordinary session.

ARTICLE XIII

The Council of Ministers shall be responsible to the Assembly of Heads of State and Government. It shall be entrusted with the responsibility of preparing conferences of the Assembly.

It shall take cognisance of any matter referred to it by the Assembly. It shall be entrusted with the implementation of the decision of the Assembly of Heads of State and Government. It shall co-ordinate inter-African co-operation in accordance with the instructions of the Assembly and in conformity with Article II (2) of the present Charter.

ARTICLE XIV

1. Each Member State shall have one vote.
2. All resolutions shall be determined by a simple majority of the Council of Ministers.

3. Two-thirds of the total membership of the Council shall form a quorum for any meeting of the Council.

ARTICLE XV

The Council shall have the power to determine its own rule of procedure.

GENERAL SECRETARIAT

ARTICLE XVI

There shall be an administrative Secretary-General of the Organization, who shall be appointed by the Assembly of Heads of State and Government, on the recommendation of the Council of Ministers. The Administrative Secretary-General shall direct the affairs of the Secretariat.

ARTICLE XVII

There shall be one or more Assistant Secretaries-General of the Organization, who shall be appointed by the Assembly of Heads of State and Government.

ARTICLE XVIII

The function and condition of service of the Secretary-General and the Assistant Secretaries-General and other employees of the Secretariat shall be governed by the provisions of this Charter and the regulations approved by the Assembly of Heads of State and Government.

(1) In the performance of their duties the Administrative Secretary-General and the staff shall not seek or receive instructions from any Government or from any other authority external to the Organ-

ization. They shall refrain from any action which might reflect on their position as international officials responsible only to the Organization.

(2) Each Member of the Organization undertakes to respect the exclusive character of the responsibilities of the Administrative Secretary-General and the staff and not to seek to influence them in the discharge of their responsibilities.

COMMISSION OF MEDIATION, CONCILIATION AND ARBITRATION

ARTICLE XIX

Member States pledge to settle all disputes among themselves by peaceful means and, to this end, decide to establish a Commission of Mediation, Conciliation and Arbitration, the composition of which and the condition of service shall be defined by a separate protocol to be approved by the Assembly of Heads of State and Government.

SPECIALIZED COMMISSIONS

ARTICLE XX

The Assembly shall establish such Specialized Commissions as it may deem necessary, including the following:

(1) Economic and Social Commission;
(2) Educational and Cultural Commission;
(3) Health, Sanitation and Nutrition Commission;
(4) Defence Commission;
(5) Scientific, Technical and Research Commission.

ARTICLE XXI

Each Specialized Commission referred to in Article XX shall be composed of the Ministers concerned or other Ministers or Plenipotentiaries designated by the Governments of the Member States.

ARTICLE XXII

The functions of the Specialized Commissions shall be carried out in accordance with the provisions of the present Charter and of the regulations approved by the Council of Ministers.

THE BUDGET

ARTICLE XXIII

The budget of the Organization prepared by the Administrative Secretary-General shall be approved by the Council of Ministers. The budget shall be provided by contributions from Member States in accordance with the scale of assessment of the United Nations; provided, however, that no Member State shall be assessed an amount exceeding twenty per cent. of the yearly regular budget of the Organization. The Member States agree to pay their respective contributions regularly.

SIGNATURE AND RATIFICATION OF CHARTER

ARTICLE XXIV

This Charter shall be open for signature to all independent sovereign African States and shall be ratified by the signatory States in accordance with their respective constitutional processes.

The original instrument, done, if possible in African languages, in English and French, all texts being equally authentic, shall be deposited with the Government of Ethiopia which shall transmit certified copies thereof to all independent sovereign African States.

Instruments of ratification shall be deposited with the Government of Ethiopia, which shall notify all signatories of each such deposit.

ENTRY INTO FORCE

ARTICLE XXV

This Charter shall enter into force immediately upon receipt by the Government of Ethiopia of the instruments of ratification from two-thirds of the signatory States.

REGISTRATION OF THE CHARTER

ARTICLE XXVI

This Charter shall, after due ratification, be registered with the Secretariat of the United Nations through the Government of Ethiopia, in conformity with Article 102 of the Charter of the United Nations.

INTERPRETATION OF THE CHARTER

ARTICLE XXVII

Any question which may arise concerning the interpretation of this Charter shall be decided by a vote of two-thirds of the Assembly of Heads of State and Government of the Organization.

ADHESION AND ACCESSION

ARTICLE XXVIII

1. Any independent sovereign African State may at any time notify the Administrative Secretary-General of its intention to adhere or accede to this Charter.

2. The Administrative Secretary-General shall, on receipt of such notification, communicate a copy of it to all the Member States. Admission shall be decided by a simple majority of the Member States. The decision of each Member State shall be transmitted to the Administrative Secretary-General, who shall, upon receipt of the required number of votes, communicate the decision to the State concerned.

MISCELLANEOUS

ARTICLE XXIX

The working languages of the Organization and all its institutions shall be, if possible, African languages, English and French.

ARTICLE XXX

The Administrative Secretary-General may accept on behalf of the Organization gifts, bequests and other donations made to the Organization, provided that this is approved by the Council of Ministers.

ARTICLE XXXI

The Council of Ministers shall decide on the privileges and immunities to be accorded to the personnel of the

Secretariat in the respective territories of the Member States.

CESSATION OF MEMBERSHIP

ARTICLE XXXII

Any State which desires to renounce its membership shall forward a written notification to the Administrative Secretary-General. At the end of one year from the date of such notification, if not withdrawn, the Charter shall cease to apply with respect to the renouncing State, which shall thereby cease to belong to the Organization.

AMENDMENT TO THE CHARTER

ARTICLE XXXIII

This Charter may be amended or revised if any Member State makes a written request to the Administrative Secretary-General to that effect; provided, however, that the proposed amendment is not submitted to the Assembly for consideration until all the Member States have been duly notified of it and a period of one year has elapsed. Such an amendment shall not be effective unless approved by at least two-thirds of all the Member States.

In faith whereof, We, the Heads of African States and Governments, have signed this Charter.

Done in the City of Addis Ababa, this 25th day of May, 1963.